Effective Time Management

Personnel, Guidance, and Management Series

Alternative Higher Education

Systems Change Strategies in Educational Settings
Arends, R.I., Ph.D. and Arends, J.H., Ph.D.

Counseling in Correctional Environments
Bennett, L.A., and Rosenbaum, T.S.

Current Issues and Strategies in Organization Development
Burke, W.W., Ph.D.

Effective Time Management: A Practical Workbook
Davidson, J.

Structured Groups for Facilitating Development
Drum, D.J., Ph.D. and Knott, J.E., Ph.D.

New Career Options for Women
Farmer, H.S., Ph.D. and Backer, T.E. Ph.D.

New Methods for Delivering Human Services
Jones, G.B., Ph.D., Dayton, C., Ph.D. and Gelatt, H.B., Ph.D.

The Guidance Counselor as Sex Educator
SIECUS

Women in the Work Force
Katzell, M.E., Ph.D. and Byham, W.C., Ph.D. (eds)

Parent Education and Elementary Counseling
Lamb, J., Ph.D. and Lamb, W., Ph.D.

Industrial Mental Health and Employee Counseling
Noland, R.L., Ph.D. (ed.)

Counseling Older Persons
Sinick, D. Ph.D.

Mental Health Related Activities of Companies and Unions
Slotkin, E.J., M.A., et. al.

New Approaches to College Student Development
Tollefson, A.L., Ph.D.

Effective Time Management
A Practical Workbook

Jim Davidson
People in Business, Manassas, Virginia

HUMAN SCIENCES PRESS
72 Fifth Avenue   3 Henrietta Street
NEW YORK, NY 10011 ● LONDON, WC2E 8LU

Library of Congress Catalog Number 78-6126

ISBN: 0-87705-332-4

Copyright © 1978 by Human Sciences Press 72 Fifth Avenue, New York, New York 10011

All rights reserved. No part of this work may be reproduced or utilized in any form or by any means, electronic or mechanical, including photocopying, microfilm and recording, or by any information storage and retrieval system without permission in writing from the publisher.

Printed in the United States of America
89 987654321

Library of Congress Cataloging in Publication Data

    Davidson, Jim.
        Effective time management.

        Bibliography: p.
        1. Time allocation. 2. Management. I. Title.
        II. Title: Time management.
HD38.D29   658.4   78-6126
IBSN 0-87705-332-4

Contents

PREFACE 7

SECTION 1. TECHNIQUES 9
   1. Have You Good Reason to Manage Your Time Effectively? 11
   2. How to Manage Your Day Effectively 13
   3. The 5-Minute Priority Setting Conference 22
   4. How to Block Interruptions 24
   5. How to Reduce Length of Meetings 36
   6. What About Flexitime? 41
   7. How to Help Individual Staff Members with Their Time Management 46
   8. How Your Total Office/Company Can Increase Productivity by 10 to 30% 49

SECTION 2. BEHAVIOR 67
   9. Why People Mismanage Time 69
  10. How to Counteract Procrastination 75
  11. Work Habits and Their Effect on Time Structuring 80
  12. Assertive Behavior as a Time Saver 90
  13. The Need for a Positive Work Atmosphere 95

Preface

Time is an invaluable resource. When time is not utilized effectively, productivity and money are automatically lost. How you arrange your time is how you arrange your life, and in your business, managing time is often synonymous with managing the job.

Skills are needed to manage effectively. There really isn't any such thing as a "born" manager or a "born" salesman. It is true that some people show more promise than others in being effective, but they all need skills, and the more workable skills a manager has at his or her fingertips, the more he or she is able to accomplish the job successfully. The following pages are filled with time-managing ideas to add to your existing skills.

The first section concentrates on techniques in managing time. These are practical items such as "Have an agenda for each meeting," or "Have a priority-setting conference with your secretary early in the day." These techniques are practices that are well proven. The second section concentrates on the behavioral aspects of managing time. Here we approach less tangible items such as "Why do I procrastinate?" or "How can I win the support of the rest of my staff so that we can work more effectively with each other?" Techniques are easier to understand because they are more concrete and more measurable than the behavioral aspects. Yet, without the proper behavior that accompanies putting these techniques into operation, little might be accomplished. We talk about "skills" training today meaning techniques only. I refuse, however, to think of behavioral performance as being nonskills training. I see communication, self-examination, and self-assertion as highly sensitive skills to be learned and perfected. They don't come naturally.

If we are to make full use of our time we need to learn what to do (techniques) and how to make it all happen for ourselves and others (behavior).

Jim Davidson

CHAPTER 1

HAVE YOU GOOD REASON TO MANAGE YOUR TIME EFFECTIVELY?

A secretary attended a time management workshop and told the instructor: "I'm not getting much out of this course." The instructor probed a little deeper and discovered that the secretary had worked only 90 minutes during the previous day. The rest of the time was spent in the cafeteria and talking with people in other offices. The secretary wanted to stretch work, not condense it! She attended the workshop to fill up the day!

We do not manage our time well until we have good reason to do so. The manager who has not recognized that *time* and *people* (I think they are of equal value) are his or her most valuable resources, is not likely to work at making better use of his or her 8-hour day.

Three preliminary questions need to be asked. The answers will help you to assess at the outset what kind of motivation you have for this workshop.

Question 1. *If you could condense your present 8-hour-a-day job into 7 hours, what would you do with the extra hour?* The manager who has little to do finds this question nonsensical. The busy manager who creates work just to look important will not be enthralled with the answer. The creative manager will be really glad to speculate what could be done with that extra hour. He or she senses accomplishment and is eager to save that one hour.

Question 2. *If you could do more in less time how do you think you would feel about yourself?* It is important for the manager to feel well about him- or herself in accomplishing. Be specific. "Good" is a general answer that is quite vague, whereas "I would feel like I was progressing and getting closer to my goals" would be more specific.

Question 3. *Would managing time better contribute toward your promotion?* Most people desire promotion. The answer to this question leads to another question: "Will the manager responsible for my yearly performance appraisal give me a better report if I do more in less time?" The answer to this may not always be

SECTION 1—TECHNIQUES

"Yes," although it looks like it should be. However, the manager should know whether or not he or she will personally benefit with a reward as a result of better time management.

YOUR ANSWER TO QUESTION 1.

YOUR ANSWER TO QUESTION 2.

YOUR ANSWER TO QUESTION 3.

CHAPTER 2
HOW TO MANAGE YOUR DAY EFFECTIVELY

To manage means to have a system—and it helps if the system works! In this chapter a system is outlined that many managers use in one form or another and have found to be successful. As you work it each day it will take you no more than 10 minutes. Since I have used it I have put my 8-hour day into between 6½ and 7 hours. This is a considerable savings! This does not mean you will experience the same, because it depends on how well (or poorly) you are functioning at present. It also depends on the nature of your job. The more permission you have to order your own day's work, the more need you have for a system like this and the more hours will be saved compared with the manager or salesperson whose day is largely mapped out by someone else.

Before arriving at daily planning, three quick—but important—steps must be taken in order to give context to the daily scheduling.

1. *Determine what you would like to see happening between now and this time next year.* This could range from wanting to have a better relationship with your staff, to being in another job position or to making 15% more sales than you made last year. You might have only 1 desire for the next year, but, then again, you might have 10. If you have several, number them in order of importance. If one of your desires seems unattainable, don't cross it out, simply adjust it. For example, if you want to be a member of the board of directors next year, and that looks extremely unlikely, you can serve in a capacity that will help you realize your desire sooner than you think. Take a specific but realistic step in the process of having your desire fulfilled.

It is extremely important to be in touch with what we desire from our jobs and to work at fulfilling these desires wholly or partially. If we don't, we have little self-direction and, more than likely, we will feel frustrated and unfulfilled in our employment. Besides, we tend to be more productive working on a project that we like.

In determining what you want, realize your own priorities. This means that, in your day-to-day scheduling, you have to give energy and time to fulfilling these priorities, otherwise you will be fulfilling others' priorities at the expense of your own.

2. *Determine what your division or section would like to see happening between now and this time next year.* Your division or section could be embodied in one single person, perhaps your chief supervisor. We are talking here about the person or group that determines the central direction and goals of the organization; for example, a government division's central aim over the next few months might be to educate the general public about some health hazard, or a sales organization might want to put a new product on the market.

Once you have determined this you have set your division's priorities. If you are unclear about them I suggest you find out!

You now have two sets of priorities—your own and your division's. You are on your way to seeing that the majority of your time needs to be spent in fulfilling these priorities. Perhaps your priorities are the same as the division's—no problem. If they are different, but not in conflict, you have to work out how both sets of priorities can be given adequate attention. If the two sets of priorities are in conflict then a decision has to be reached to resolve the matter. In the final analysis, if a manager cannot fulfill the priorities of the organization, and he or she has been unsuccessful in changing those priorities, that manager might be more productive working in a situation where his or her own desires and the wishes of the organization were closely compatible.

3. *Determine the present and imminent priority projects in your division that involve you.* For example, during the next 5 weeks next year's budget will need to be finalized, or a special report has to be prepared for the marketing division. These are projects that are essential to the total welfare of the organization and that directly or indirectly serve in fulfilling its goals. Some of these priorities are constant, such as a government employee who finds little variation in the priority of answering letters of complaint received from the public.

My goals for the next year.

Practical ways to accomplish the three most important goals.

My division's goals for the next year.

My practical involvement with the division's goals.

Current priorities in my job.

In establishing your own wants, the organization's goals, and the current priorities in your job, you will have identified those areas in which you will have to spend most of your time and energy. Time consumed in your working day on items that do not serve these wants and priorities is, for the most part, wasted time. This does not mean there is no place for a coffee break or other forms of relaxation. For most of us these are essential in performing a better job.

You are now ready for the day-to-day process in which you plan and utilize your time. Following are five simple and quick steps that will take you about 10 minutes each day to complete, but the result could save up to 2 hours a day. These steps consist of identifying work items, setting priorities, delegating duties, and making full use of your calendar. As you proceed through these steps, keep referring to page 00 to see how you can use the daily worksheet more clearly.

STEP 1, Identify work items

Make a list of items that could possibly be done today and also items that you want to do in the near future. In this space on your worksheet record everything you can think of on this one list. Do not trust your memory. There is something you will forget and you will burn up energy trying to remember what it is. The only thing you should remember now is to consult your list! The items should include large and small projects, items that are time consuming, as well as items that take only a minute to perform. Be specific; for example, "phone calls" is too general. If there are many calls to be made, categorize them or identify them by using the names of the people you are calling.

STEP 2, Go over your list and pull out any items that need to be broken down

Most of these items are lengthy but some only take an hour or two to do, but nevertheless could have five or more components. Preparing a report could involve going to the library, talking with Mary, consulting the last report, checking some figures with the finance department, and finding out the deadline date. The whole report could be completed in 90 minutes including all the preliminary work, but the breakdown could be helpful from many angles. For example, Mary is hard to track down sometimes so with the breakdown it may become evident that Mary better be sought out first. Her information is needed for the latter part of the report. Without the breakdown, I would probably try to get hold of her near the end of my project—then she is not to be found and the report is held back for another day.

STEP 3, Evaluate your work items and your breakdown list

Look at every item you have before you and ask yourself this: *"If nothing else should get done today, what is the one item that must be done?"* Some days that is easy to answer. A salesperson looks at his or her list one day and it is clear what customer it is essential to see. The next day the salesperson sees three items that are "musts." At that point it is important to choose one of these three to tackle first, otherwise indecision may lead to tackling them all at once and finalizing nothing by the end of the day.

This one item becomes your *Ace* for the day. Jot it down under "Ace" on your worksheet and cross it off your list.

Now identify other items on your list that are very important and that you would like to accomplish today. Be realistic. It will not serve any purpose to identify items that would take you 20 hours to do. Pick out only the very important issues and the ones that need to be accomplished imminently. These are now your *Kings* (or Queens). Jot them down in order of importance under "Kings" in your worksheet and cross them off your list. If it's at all possible you will want to complete your Ace before embarking on your Kings. Sometimes your Ace cannot be performed first thing in the morning; for example, my Ace today might be to see McDonald about a contract but he won't be back in town until 2:00 P.M.

You now have important items to be accomplished today. They have to be worked into your schedule and interruptions must be kept at bay as much as possible (see Chapter 3). For some time now time management specialists have emphasized the importance of not overscheduling. It is impractical to schedule every minute of the day. Depending on interruptions, your availability to subordinates, and other normal unexpected projects imposed on you, you will want to select only the items that could possibily be achieved that day.

You now have two categories of items left on your list. You have important items that you think you will not be able to do today, but you might if you have time. These are your *Jacks*. Then you have other items that are not important and would not serve goals and priorities. These are your *Deuces*. Jot the Jacks in the Jack column, but only the ones you might want to do today if there is time. The other Jacks get transferred to future worksheets. For example, preparation of the budget figures are not needed for another 6 weeks. There are certainly more pressing things to do today. You might think, I don't need to make a breakdown list today, but I certainly will have to do it and start on an aspect of it soon. What I need to do now is select a day when I will start on the budget and make sure I leave enough time for completion. So I select a week from today. I then turn to my worksheet for this day next week and put it on my list of things to do. I then cross it off today's list. This particular Jack is not for today but it could be my Ace next week.

In most cases most of your Jacks will be put on your list for the next two or three days, depending on their order of importance.

Deuces aren't worth the time for you and should be forgotten or put on your list under Deuces if they are important to other people, or if they are little things that could be dealt with quickly to make life more pleasant; for example, "Ask Nellie to make the coffee a little stronger!" Only list under *Deuces* in your worksheet if you think it might be some value to someone. Remember, however, Deuces are not important to you and they do not serve goals.

STEP 4, Delegate whatever you can

As a manager, you have heard about delegation from many quarters. I became so used to the term that it has lost its magic. However, although the term is a bit worn the concept still has its worth. Even many effective managers are not delegating and controlling enough of their work. It is so easy to do the tasks yourself that others are doing. This is particularly true of managers who have not been trained to be managers, for example, technicians who have graduated into management. They have been so used to "doing" that they are not able to delegate these jobs to others. Go over your Ace, Kings, and Jacks (and Deuce if applicable) and pick out all the elements that others on the staff could be doing. Go over these items *with a fine-tooth comb* and jot down the delegatable items, or parts of items, under "Delegation" in your worksheet. You are now ready to delegate work to the people concerned as quickly as possible.

STEP 5, Identify your high productivity hours and plan your calendar accordingly

The first part of this last step can be determined immediately, whereas all the other steps need to be performed at the beginning of each working day.

To identify your high productivity hours ask yourself: "In my working day, when am I most mentally alert?" This is to help you determine the period of day in which you are able to concentrate with a clear mind. There may be one period (e.g., between 8:30 A.M. and 11:30 A.M.) or two or more periods (e.g., between 8:00 A.M. and 10:00 A.M. and between 2:00 P.M. and 4:00 P.M.). So far, in my inquiries at workshops, I have not yet discovered anyone who functions with full clarity and alertness for the whole working day. That is not to say that such people do not exist, but if they do, they are rare!

During your high productivity hours you should deal with your Ace and Kings, particularly those that demand the greatest concentration. When possible, leave the less important jobs to the time when you do not function as well. You want to guard your high productivity hours against every unnecessary interruption.

Now that you know when you function best, move your Ace and Kings over into your calendar. Work on the appointment system for yourself and also in your dealings with others as much as possible. The more you schedule, the fewer the interruptions.

We have reached a point in our process that looks neat and tidy but has an appearance of unreality. After all, as a first-line manager, I would receive a call from my boss at 11:00 A.M. demanding a project to be completed that day. My Ace is now in jeopardy and my Kings are blown sky high. This happens all too often. Some of these interventions can be curbed while others are unavoidable. That's the name of the game. Problems are here to stay. When this happens, your day needs to be rescheduled quickly. The boss has given you a new Ace perhaps. Hopefully you will be able to accomplish your own Ace that day also. There are days that are chaotic, a series of putting out fires, for instance. Thankfully not every day is like this, otherwise no constructive work could ever be done. Because there are many extenuating circumstances that eat into our time, there is all the more reason to set priorities and plan the time that we do have to ourselves, even if it does mean rescheduling. I have worked with hundreds of supervisors in the federal government who receive myriad requests from Washington, D.C., or their State Office. When a request is issued by an executive in Washington to a particular supervisor he or she has no idea how many other requests that supervisor is receiving that day from other sources. The result is often utter frustration for the supervisor, who feels he or she must meet all the demands. Here is an instance in which this supervisor must determine the Ace and the Kings and go home at night having left work undone and be able to say, "I did the best job possible given this chaotic situation. The world will not come to an end because some of my Kings that I chose this morning will need to wait until tomorrow."

To be safe, the supervisor may have to contact his or her own manager, explain what is happening, and bring the boss into the decision-making process as to what receives attention first. This means that when a call comes through from an important figure asking why a request has not yet been met, the supervisor has support from higher sources. Whenever a supervisor is swamped with demands that all look like Aces, he or she is generally not wise to go it alone. The support of a higher-positioned person is needed either to give the supervisor "carte blanche" to set the priorities or to have that higher-positioned person participate in setting the priority. This is not clearly defined in many organizations and the "blaming" game results all too often.

20 SECTION 1–TECHNIQUES

ITEMS TO DO		EARLY MORNING
Staff Mtg. office furniture (Jan. 9) Report to John Budget Mtg. Customers letters (6) Phone Mary Agenda for district mtg. Atlanta material red pencils Plane tickets Sign check Project B		8:00 8:15 — Priority 8:30 conference 8:45 9:00 9:15 — Ace 9:30 9:45 10:00 10:15 10:30 ⎤ 10:45 Kings 11:00 1, 2, 3 + 5 11:15 11:30 ⎦ 11:45
	DELEGATE TO	12:00 12:15 — Lunch 12:30 w/ Arnold 12:45
A ♣ Atlanta material prep.		1:00 ⎤ Preliminary 1:15 Budget Mtg. 1:30 ⎦

K ♣   1. Dist. Mtg. Agenda — Bob
2. Letters
3. Budget Mtg.
    – lost file
    – estimates — Marge
    – present spending
4. Staff Mtg.
5. Sign Checks
6. Project B
		1:45 ⎤
		2:00 Project B
		2:15
		2:30 ⎦
		2:45
		3:00
		3:15 — Staff Mtg.
		3:30
		3:45
		4:00 — Checks
		4:15
		4:30
		4:45
		5:00

J ♣ Plane tickets Phone Mary Report to John		**LATE AFTERNOON**
2 ♣ Red pencils	Marge	

MAKE A LIST OF ALL THE ITEMS YOU ANTICIPATE WILL BE WAITING FOR YOU PLUS ALL THE ITEMS YOU HAVE IN MIND RIGHT NOW AND WORK THROUGH THIS SHEET USING THE FIVE STEPS OUTLINED IN THIS CHAPTER.

		DELEGATE TO	EARLY MORNING
A♣			8:00 8:15 8:30 8:45 9:00 9:15 9:30 9:45 10:00 10:15 10:30 10:45 11:00 11:15 11:30 11:45 12:00 12:15 12:30 12:45
K♣			1:00 1:15 1:30 1:45 2:00 2:15 2:30 2:45
J♣			3:00 3:15 3:30 3:45 4:00 4:15 4:30 4:45 5:00
2♣			**LATE AFTERNOON**

CHAPTER 3
THE 5-MINUTE PRIORITY SETTING CONFERENCE

Having set your priorities for the day, it is likely that other people will be involved as you start executing your tasks. If others on your staff are also practicing a priority-setting method, they too will have to contact the manager and other staff members. So this leads us to the 5-minute priority setting conference. This conference could take place about 20 minutes after people have arrived at work. This gives them time to make their list for the day. At a set time then, manager and staff meet together to let each other know what they are going to be doing and where they are going to be for most of the day. The secretary is given the items for the day from the manager. This enables the secretary to plan. If a secretary is working for two or more managers, he or she can hear what items are important from each manager. If the secretary sees too much work coming, then he or she has the opportunity to ask which tasks should be done first. The managers must decide so that the secretary is not the decision maker. Not only do high priority items get accomplished by this method, potential problems are warded off. For example, let's say the secretary is busy and getting work done by 4:30 P.M. It is 3:15 P.M. and one of the managers comes with a lengthy report to be typed. The secretary has to refuse to do it or else cut out another manager's work to do the report. This could easily lead to conflict. The priority setting conference eliminates a great deal of this kind of conflict.

There are two essential elements for this conference: (1) It should remain a priority setting conference. It must not turn into a staff meeting. (2) It should be limited to 5 minutes. This means everyone present needs to be standing. It should be held in a room with no chairs!

Identify the person(s) you must confer with at the beginning of each day.

What benefits do you think would occur if you had this priority setting conference each day? Are there any problems that might be reduced?

Would there be any disadvantages, and if so, how could they be met?

CHAPTER 4

HOW TO BLOCK INTERRUPTIONS

What can be done with open door and open space practices

According to a recent study, the average manager in the United States is interrupted an average of every 8 minutes. A visitor drops by, the boss buzzes on the intercom, a phone call, plus many other happenings make it extremely difficult for the manager to maintain concentration for any length of time. Managers say that because of constant interruptions—some important, but most quite unimportant— only 2 hours of essential work is accomplished in an 8-hour day. That is staggering! This results in low productivity if the company or the manager works overtime, cutting into hours needed for recreation and family.

Over the past 20 years we have been moving steadily in two directions that have tended to multiply our time management problems. These are the open door and open space policies. In the open door policy, managers should be available to subordinates throughout the working day. It came about gradually but accelerated in the 1960s, the decade of the promotion of human rights. Favorable working conditions, numerous benefits, equal rights, and the emergence of participatory management are only a few ideas surrounding the movement to promote the importance and dignity of the person in the working situation. The open door policy adopted by many organizations is an outcome of this emphasis to show that people are important. To reduce the tension between the needs of people and productivity is not an easy task. Often, managers who refuse to see their subordinates on demand are branded as unsympathetic whereas those who see their staff at all times end up frustrated through not having enough time to accomplish their own tasks.

The key word to describe the open door policy is "availability."

The open space policy has resulted mainly from economic and environmental pressures. Space means money, and a great deal of money if the office is located in the downtown business section of the city. Private offices are increasingly coveted by managers but unavailable to the majority. More and more companies are utilizing space by having employees located in large areas, sometimes accommodating scores of people. Movable partitions are sometimes employed to provide a measure of privacy. However, the overall effect is that people are now working very close together, physically, in the open space arrangement.

The cumulative effect of open door and open space policies is an increased measure of interruptions. If I am working in an atmosphere where staff members are permitted to contact me at any time and as I sit at my desk I can hear the conversation of my co-worker as he or she talks on the phone six feet away from me, the total situation is not conducive to concentration. Productivity is then threatened.

Organizations need to be productive and this is true of the federal government as well as private industry. (Government agencies seem to be particularly affected by the open door and open space practices.) Businesses exist to be productive. They exist to do a job whether selling cars, generating electricity, or making welfare payments. People are business's greatest resource and need to be treated as such, but, in the final analysis, organizations need to produce, and whatever contributes to productivity must be considered very carefully.

How then can we reduce those constant interruptions so that people can work effectively for at least part of the day? Here are three possible plans of attack; all three may be utilized simultaneously. They are model plans and can be adapted to your own organizational setting.

PLAN A—Introduce a 2-hour "quiet" time among your staff

This is a period when staff members agree not to make contact with each other in any way unless it is absolutely essential. As already indicated in Chapter 1, most people (about 95%) have a high productivity period in the morning so if it is possible the two hours should be scheduled in the morning. For example, let's take an office that begins work at 8:00 A.M. A possible schedule could be as follows:

8:00– 8:30	Preparation for the day. Brief conferences. Contact with other staff members.
8:30– 9:30	Quiet time. No internal contact between staff members.
9:30–10:30	Availability to each other. Coffee break occurs in this period.
10:30–11:30	Resumption of the quiet time.
11:30–12:00	Back to being available to each other.

Some time management experts suggest that managers work on the quarter-to-the-hour principle—that is, they will talk with support staff between a quarter to the hour and the hour. This seems unrealistic and impractical for most of us. The system outlined above is workable because it leaves six hours in the day that can be used for meetings, interviews, and other activities. During the quiet time (Q.T.), both manager and staff can concentrate on Ace and King projects, particularly those that demand concentration.

The effect of the two hours of quietness means people will save two or three items or more during these hours and so when they do come to the manager with these items they can be dealt with at the same time. This avoids multiple interruptions.

During one of the Q.T.'s you might discover you need to contact your boss. Let's say this happens at 9:00 A.M. Ask yourself: "Can it wait half an hour?" Ninety percent of the items can wait. If an emergency arises and you need to contact your boss immediately, then, of course, you will do so. All rules have exceptions.

Cooperation, good staff relations, and a spirit of teamwork are essential to the effective working of this system. It can be implemented in many ways. One suggestion that seems acceptable is to carry the idea to a staff meeting, but first of all say, "I wonder if you all have the same frustration as I have. I find there are so many interruptions I can barely think." If there is general consent that this is true then you have an opening to introduce the concept. If the staff members come up with a better solution, then you're still a winner. Most of us are slow to make changes, particularly ones that might greatly affect our normal work habits, so it is important to bring people with you, gently, in implementing such a change as this. Nothing that is done need be permanent, so if the concept does not work, it can be reversed. Implementing for a month and then reviewing it, looking at the advantages and any disadvantages, seems a safe route to take. Because there may be difficulties arising does not mean that the concept is of no value. Evaluate its worth and work through the difficulties.

PLAN B—Make yourself unavailable for phone calls part of the day

Phone calls are a constant source of interruptions for most managers, causing a break in concentration.

Hopefully, most of the calls are work related so they are not irrelevant, but if, during the 2-hour Q.T. for the staff, phone calls were handled by a clerk-typist or a secretary and only the very important ones were accepted, then the manager is disturbed even less for part of the day. Since in most offices 80% of the calls come from 20% of the callers, that 20% could be asked not to phone during these two hours. Here is a technique that seems to work well: "John, we are terribly behind in our work here and we are trying to cut down on visitors and phone calls for a period to enable us to concentrate on some priority projects. I wonder if you could delay phoning each day until 11 o'clock." If the office has a policy in effect then it is easier. The caller can be notified of the policy and this makes it much less of a personal issue.

HOW TO BLOCK INTERRUPTIONS 27

The key person is, of course, the one answering the phones. That person has to be informative and try to find out the nature of the call. If he or she says the manager will return the call later in the day then the manager should do so to retain credibility.

If quiet time is not consistently observed the manager needs to inform the secretary to hold all calls while he or she works on important projects. Very often you hear, "I'm sorry, he's in a meeting just now." That seems a good reason for not being disturbed, but when the manager is at his or her desk working steadily he or she might be accomplishing much more than what would be accomplished in the meeting. Why should the manager be available simply because he or she is in the office? It doesn't make sense. The secretary can simply say, "Mr. Jones is not available until 10:30. Will you call back then?" "Not available" can mean anything from Mr. Jones being out of the office to sitting in his office working on his Ace project. There is no need for the secretary to give any more information (unless it's the president calling from the head office).

PLAN C—Make yourself unavailable to visitors part of the day

Visitors, like staff workers and phone calls, are a source of interruption if they arrive on your doorstep when you are giving serious thought to a King item. The intrusion of a visitor at this point breaks your concentration and puts you another 20 minutes or half an hour behind schedule.

If the quiet period is in operation then it makes sense to keep visitors away during that time. This would mean you could have a 2-hour period in the morning entirely for yourself with minimal interruptions.

To keep visitors from just dropping in, you need to inform people you won't be "dropped in on." This means appointments need to be made. When a manager works on the appointment system, nobody has any cause to complain when someone "drops in" and the manager will not see the person.

In a recent seminar one participant told how in the open space office he is easily seen at his desk whenever anyone drops in to have a conference with him. Assertiveness comes in handy in such instances. The visitor needs to be told by the secretary that the manager is working on an important item and won't be free for an hour. The other way is to have a 6-foot-high movable partition placed between the manager and the office door, then nobody can see the manager sitting there. This can be quite effective.

Blocking out time for yourself saves time. Around 30% more productivity is gained by having a period without interruptions.

28 SECTION 1—TECHNIQUES

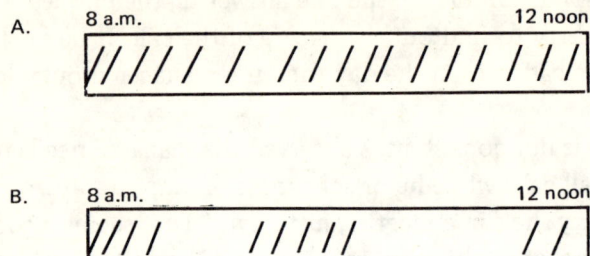

Diagram A above indicates that the manager was interrupted 17 times in a 4-hour period by phones, staff, and unscheduled visitors. Diagram B indicates 2 hours of no interruptions under the steps outlined in this chapter. This total number of interruptions amount to 11. On this system the staff saves questions and presents them at one time, thus cutting down on the number of contacts. Productivity in the case of B can be 30% over the productivity of A.

How to keep your Q.T. alive. By operating Plans A, B, and C for one or more hours a day, you and your staff accomplish more work. The percentage will vary but your productivity will go up. However, we humans can easily slip into our old ways, so the effectiveness of the operation needs to be evaluated at least once a month, possibly at the staff meetings. Praise needs to be given to all who cooperate and successes need to be noted. If any aspect of the plan is falling behind or any problems are resulting, these should be addressed seriously. Putting a Q.T. into operation and maintaining it is not easy, but when people get the message and see its benefits, they will help you keep it going.

Q.T. doesn't work in all situations. Where people constantly need each other or when an office has as its function serving the public 8 hours a day (e.g., welfare office or auto claims section) some people could not enjoy its benefits in the form outlined above. However, the same principles can often be employed. In one office four people answered the phones and met the public 8 hours a day. They were also supposed to process orders, but orders were being processed very slowly. A consultant friend of mine made the suggestion to the company that for a 3-hour period each day one of the four workers do nothing else but process orders. The result was a 33% increase in the speed of delivery. This was a simple move. In essence, one person each day was permitted to have a Q.T. to process the orders.

The secretary's Q.T. The support person who has intercepted visitors and phone calls during the office Q.T. may have accomplished very little typing or filing or whatever, and in some organizations the secretary is very busy, perhaps serving four managers or more. This means in order for the secretary to execute the manager's work he or she needs to be protected from interruptions. The secretary could have a period in the afternoon when the managers or other staff members could answer the phones instead of him or her, thus freeeing the secretary for his or her own Ace and Kings.

Below are two letters sent out by a branch chief in the Department of Commerce. They illustrate a practical implementation of the quiet-time concept and reveal difficulties and benefits for that particular office. The first letter with the rules was sent out after the concept had been discussed and general agreement was reached. There was a 6-week period between the first and second letters. The temporary termination of the Q.T. was due to the slack period that office experienced in the summer months.

FIRST LETTER

SUBJECT: Experimental Quiet Time

Management studies have found that most individuals are more productive in their morning hours. In a recent time management class, the concept of controlling employee interruptions during recognized high-productivity periods was cited as a means to increase employee performance and job production. This concept is to be introduced on a trial basis in the Requirements Branch. Effective May 9, 1977, between the hours of 8:30 and 9:30 A.M., attempts will be made to eliminate all internally and externally caused interruptions so as to minimize their normally negative effects on employee performance. These job interruptions, usually in the form of routine visits and telephone calls from other agency personnel, will be intercepted by designated Branch personnel and rescheduled for proper response at a later hour. All "emergency" business matters will be responded to immediately, however, so as not to create undesirable negative effects on this management program.

It is not the intent of this experiment to shut out those whose cooperation is so vital to our work, but rather to schedule them around a block of time during which we can concentrate on our own requirements. Comments on this trial, both prior to its adoption and after it has been in operation, are welcome. If some facet is not consistent with your requirements, please advise me accordingly.

QUIET TIME RULES

1. All interruptions, both internal and external, will be absolutely minimal.
2. The door to room 408 will be closed during the "quiet" time.
3. Only emergency visits or phone calls will be accepted. For purposes of this program those ranking as Captains, or their equivalents, and higher shall be defined as automatic emergencies. Phone calls from outside NOS (National Oceanic Survey) or long-distance calls will be accepted.
4. Telephone answering duties will be rotated among Requirements Branch staff during the "quiet" time.
5. Outgoing calls will be allowed, but conversations should be brief and subdued.

SECOND LETTER

SUBJECT: Quiet Time Report

Effective June 14, 1977, the Requirements Branch will no longer be observing a quiet time. Termination of this experiment does not indicate the period to be without value, but rather is due to changed circumstances in the workload of the branch. It is anticipated that the quiet time will be reinstated this fall, probably in October. Your co-operation during the experiment was excellent.

The quiet time was found to be very beneficial in allowing uninterrupted work time. When coupled with flexitime, it could amount to as much as 2½ hours of disturbance-free time for employees. This time can be used for concentrated work. If the infrequent interruptions experienced are indicative of general circumstances, very few interruptions are of such an emergency nature that they cannot be postponed.

During our quiet time, the door to the branch was closed with an explanatory sign. Although we had originally planned to reschedule all telephone calls, this proved awkward. Therefore, telephone calls were accepted after the first week. Responsibility for answering the telephone was rotated among branch personnel; thereby, the branch secretary also was able to work without interruptions. The greatest problem arising during the quiet time was internal interruptions. It seems that people find it very difficult to remain quiet. Ideally, questions or comments would be held until after the quiet time. When the period is reinstated, this is an area for increased effort.

In summary, the implementation of a quiet time proved to be an effective management tool and present plans call for its future use. If there are any questions concerning the plan, its benefits, or its problems, feel free to call me.

The other time robbers

In most offices, constant internal contact with other employees, phone calls, and visitors come up on top of the list of time robbers. But there are more, and plenty of them. Here is a typical list.

- Unclear information
- Lack of information
- Voluminous reading material
- Unscheduled meetings
- Large staff turnover
- Unavailability of people
- Circulating junk mail
- Complicated filing system
- Missing files
- Pastime conversations

- Unnecessary meetings
- Prolonged breaks
- Lack of support staff
- Inadequate premises
- Red tape
- Mistakes
- Waiting for a signature
- Mechanical failures
- Undefined roles
- Background music
- Missing staff member

HOW TO BLOCK INTERRUPTIONS   31

Now make your own list of the time robbers you encounter in your work.

Pick out the five most time-consuming items. Go around the group and gather suggestions to help solve these problems. If a suggestion sounds crazy—put it down anyway. It may prove to be the best. Do this for 15 minutes.

	ITEM	SUGGESTIONS
1.		
2.		
3.		
4.		
5.		

TIME MANAGEMENT CASE STUDY

After reading the following case carefully, rewrite Donald's morning to see if he had applied time managing techniques that you have learned in this workshop. He worked a 4-hour morning and still had essential work left over. Use your imagination. You can make reasonable assumptions. Use the two blank pages following this case for analysis and new schedule.

8:00   Donald is a middle manager; he arrives on time. Pours himself a cup of coffee. Picks up secretary's *Washington Post* and reads the report of yesterday's Redskins game. Chats with secretary, Sally, about the farewell party for Jones to take place this afternoon.

8:20   Phone rings. Call from head office to have Donald send financial statistics to help compile next year's budget. Donald is told to get the figures over as soon as possible.

8:30   Angela, a colleague, comes in and talks with Donald about the effect the new administration will have on their work. The conversation leads them to talk about a TV program that they both saw recently.

8:45   A clerk typist comes in with papers she has photocopied. Angela excuses herself. Donald thumbs through the papers to make sure everything is O.K. He notices a paper that needs rewording so he rewrites it while the clerk typist stands and waits. He instructs her to retype the page and have copies made. This item had to do with information a customer had requested for his interest. It was not pressing but looked like it was important.

9:05   Phone rings. Secretary tells him it is Arnold, his immediate boss, who wants to see him right away for a report on yesterday's meeting. Goes to Arnold's office and remains there discussing meeting until 9:45. Donald has still to write up the report for Arnold.

9:45   Returns to his office. Thinks about various items to be done. About eight come to mind. Feels "there aren't enough hours in a day." Decides he had better consult Jane and Alan about the ABC contract as it appears most pressing. He is just about to call them when—

9:55   John, a subordinate, knocks on his door (doesn't consult secretary), walks in, sits down, and proceeds to talk to him about the problem he and three other managers are having over four supervisors sharing one secretary. Donald is concerned and listens carefully. John gives a lengthy description of the proceedings, after which they discuss various solutions. John leaves, promising to try one solution but doesn't appear hopeful.

10:35   Sally brings in all the mail. Donald starts to sift mail. Asks secretary for coffee and to call Jane and Alan to get them over right away to talk about the ABC contract. He reads a catchy magazine article.

10:55   Jane arrives. Donald is sorting the mail in piles. Sally informs him that Alan will be here as soon as possible—probably another 10 minutes. Donald asks Jane to wait as he doesn't want to start the consultation without Alan. They talk about trivia while he occasionally browses through another interesting article that came in the mail.

11:05   Alan arrives. They talk about the ABC contract. Donald thought Alan and Jane would have had all the information to finalize the contract but discovers certain data is missing. Donald thought he had instructed them to have everything gathered by today, but Alan and Jane inform him they didn't hear him say this. They discuss what items still need to be looked at before finalizing the contract.

11:45   Alan and Jane leave. Secretary informs him that Clyde has been waiting to see him since 11:30 to discuss the Johnston case. Donald goes out to meet Clyde, and asks, "Did you make an appointment to see me at 11:30?" Clyde, "No, but you said on the phone yesterday you were busy and I should come to see you tomorrow morning, so here I am." Donald, "Well, I'm going to lunch. Come back at 12:45." Donald goes to lunch 15 minutes early because he has a slight headache. As Donald walks toward the cafeteria he thinks, "Heavens, that wasn't the best of mornings. I'll need to see Clyde at 12:45, and with Jones' farewell party at 3:30, that leaves me just another two hours today, and I'm supposed to finalize the ABC contract, call McKenzie, Ferrell, and Anderson, dictate about 10 letters, send the report to Arnold which was due yesterday, talk to Sally about my flight schedule, get that information to the head office, and there is no saying what other interruptions will occur. I've got enough work for two people."

For clarification, the calls to McKenzie, Ferrell, and Anderson are high priority and so are 4 of the 10 letters.

CHAPTER 5
HOW TO REDUCE LENGTH OF MEETINGS

Select a meeting you attended recently, and put a check in the "yes" or "no" column opposite each statement, based on your observations about that particular meeting.

```
                                                    YES      NO
                                                  (TRUE)  (FALSE)
```

1. The meeting needed to take place.
2. The purpose of the meeting was clear.
3. Adequate notice was given.
4. Minutes of the previous meeting were at hand.
5. I gave thought to my contributions beforehand.
6. There was a typed agenda for the meeting.
7. We kept only to items on the agenda.
8. The chairman had good control.
9. Most people attending had engaged in preparatory work.
10. A recorder was chosen.
11. I received a record of the minutes within 48 hours after the meeting.
12. Some time was saved by forming an ad hoc committee.
13. Decisions were made.
14. Everybody present needed to be there.
15. Nobody rambled or spoke just to be heard.
16. Everybody present needed to be there all of the time.
17. I needed to be there all of the time.
18. Deadlines for execution of decisions were set.
19. Important information was given.
20. It was clear who was to do what as a result of the meeting.
21. A maximum time was set for the meeting to end.

HOW TO REDUCE LENGTH OF MEETINGS

22. There was one person, other than the chairperson, who helped move the meeting along.
23. The meeting terminated on time.
24. All items on the agenda were dealt with on time.
25. Assignments from the last meeting had been fulfilled adequately.
26. The meeting was free of outside interruptions.
27. An assistant was present to deal with trivia.
28. This meeting could not have taken place in a shorter time period.
29. The time of day of the meeting was well selected.
30. Time-consuming personality clashes did not occur.

Now you are aware of some of the strengths and weaknesses of that particular meeting. Use the same 30 points for other meetings you attended recently.

When people come together anything can happen, depending on the individuals who make up the group. Meetings are places where personalities can clash and where staff members can give lengthy descriptions (which normally concern few people in the meeting) of their latest projects. Meetings are like wild horses, so if you don't put reins on them, they will run away with yours and others' time!

There are two essential elements for any kind of meeting. The first is that *every meeting needs an agenda*. An agenda is a typed list of items for discussion, unless it is a one- or two-item meeting that can be verbally communicated. The idea behind the agenda is that the chairman or someone who is appointed is given items for the meeting at least 3 hours before the meeting starts. These are put on a central list and distributed to the members before the meeting commences. The advantages are these:

1. Members know what documents to bring to the meeting.
2. Members can give thought to the items beforehand.
3. The chairman might find an item unsuitable for the meeting and avert it. For example, a staff member may bring an item to the chairman that concerns only 3 people out of 10 attending the meeting. The chairman can then direct the staff member to discuss the matter with the three separately.
4. Priorities can be set much easier on paper. When each member has an agenda in front of him or her, the person can determine what is most important. The chairman can set the priorities before the meeting or the first task of the meeting would be for the members to determine the Ace, Kings, Jacks, and Deuces.
5. Members can attend selectively. For example, on receiving the agenda, a supervisor sees only one item of concern. If the chairman sets priorities he or she can tell the supervisor roughly when to come to the meeting—perhaps after 30

minutes. If the supervisor's item is first on the list, he or she can attend the first part of the meeting and then leave.
6. The chairman need not say, "Is there anything more we need to discuss?" That is a fatal question in meetings. It is often an invitation to waste time. If an item is not on the agenda, then it doesn't get discussed. Some people like to surprise meetings with some idea that's going to take hours to discuss. The agenda system cuts this off!

The other essential element for meetings is that *every meeting needs a time limit.* For most meetings one hour is long enough. People become restless after an hour, repetition occurs frequently, and bored members begin to draw Donald Ducks and other designs on their note pads! If people traveled a long distance to attend the meeting it would be sensible to keep them there for 2 or more hours if the agenda is heavy, but with 10 minute breaks every hour.

It is a fallacy to think that decisions are better ones because everyone has participated, sometimes with lengthy discourses. Often lengthy discussion can cloud the central issue and a worse decision is made! Keep meetings short. Make a time limit and keep to it. If all the items are not covered in an hour it indicates there are too many items for one meeting or too much time being given a certain item. Here are some real benefits from a time limit.

1. A time limit has a psychological effect on the members. They tend to cut out nonessential conversation. If someone is taking a lot of time on an item, you can ask for clarification and remind him of the time limit.
2. Jacks and Deuces will be left out.
3. When an item looks like it will take some time to consider, an ad hoc committee can be formed to study the matter and report back at the next meeting. This can save hours.

Does the 1-hour meeting sound like items will be rushed and some members will go away without being heard? If so, then check this out with the members who are present. Ask if they feel rushed. My observation is that most members will be only too glad to conclude within an hour.

Here are some additional time saving tips for meetings:

Have someone to record decisions and who is to do what. He or she will then read them out at the end of the meeting so that everybody knows what has to be done. The recorder might even have these photo-copied while everyone is present and give each member a copy on leaving.

Schedule most meetings for the afternoon. We have already noted that most people function better in the morning, so allow them to do their concentrated work then. Most meetings do not demand high concentration from everyone present all the time. I have heard people coming out of a 2-hour meeting at 11:30 A.M. saying, "There goes my morning" or "I feel my day has been shot." Their productivity hours were given to discussion that a less-alert mind could have comfortably absorbed in the afternoon. If finishing time is 4:30 P.M. then put the meeting to 3:00 P.M. This gives time after the meeting to check on other items before people go home.

Start a meeting on time! If people are used to wandering in late and the meeting doesn't get underway until 10 minutes after the scheduled time, then people who were there on time were deprived for 10 minutes. When the chairperson starts on time, people soon get the message and fall into line.

Evaluate regular meetings every three months. Let's say a staff meeting takes place at 3:00 P.M. every Monday. Each quarter, take 10 minutes to critique the meeting you just had by asking these questions:

Did we start on time?
Did we accomplish what we set out to do?
Did any item take too long?
Would forming an ad hoc committee have helped?
Did everyone need to be present all the time?
What preparations could have been made which would have been helpful?

A regular evaluation of this kind helps you to keep on track.

Have some meetings standing up. If only one or two items are being discussed briefly, then brevity will not extend into longevity if there are no chairs!

Set reasonable deadlines and stick to them. When members are to follow through on a decision as a result of the meeting, it should be clear exactly when they are to be done and at which meeting a report has to be given. That report automatically goes on the agenda for that meeting. "As soon as possible" is no good.

Have lengthy reports typed up and given out to the members beforehand. In the meeting questions can be asked for clarification. People give a written report much more concisely than a verbal report.

Ask the question: "Does this meeting really need to take place at all?" Some meetings become rituals. Maybe once a month would be fine rather than every week.

When all is said and done, meetings are necessary and without them cooperation and eventually productivity would break down. Control them. Otherwise they will become monsters eating into your valuable time.

SECTION 1—TECHNIQUES

Action Plan to reduce time element in meetings I attend

(Remember, if you are not the chairman, you still have the power of suggestion.)

	ITEMS TO REDUCE TIME	LIKELY POSITIVE RESULTS	WAYS TO IMPLEMENT
E.G.	Have meeting 1½ hrs. before finishing time.	Keep conversation to the main items. Prevent lengthy unnecessary discourse. Will keep most members happy.	Talk to Bill first. Check the idea out at next meeting. Prepare reasons to change.

CHAPTER 6
WHAT ABOUT FLEXITIME?

An increasing number of private companies and federal agencies are working with flexitime. Flexitime allows, within limits, for employees to choose their own hours for work. For example, between 6:00 A.M. and 6:00 P.M. people are working in the office, only some come in at 6:00 A.M. and leave at 3:00 P.M. while others come in at 9:00 A.M. and leave at 6:00 P.M., while others again come in and leave at different hours during that time span. Each employee is at work 8 hours a day with an hour's lunch time. During this 12-hour period there is a *"core period"* when all employees are in the office. In this case the core period is 9:00 A.M. until 3:00 P.M. During the core period consultations and meetings take place. The concept behind flexitime is that people who function early in the morning can be there at work during their best productivity hours. The same goes for those who are "afternoon" people.

Within the Department of Commerce (National Oceanic and Atmospheric Administration) flexitime has been operating for several months. A questionnaire was sent out and evaluations of the experiment were tabulated. Below are some relevant aspects of the report. A total of 87 employees filled out the questionnaire, 24 of them being managers/supervisors.

One anticipated advantage of flexitime was that the number of short term sick leave occurrences (less than 8 hours) would be reduced. What has been your experience?

3	Yes, I have avoided the need to use sick leave on several occasions (10 or more times)
41	Yes, I have avoided the need to use sick leave in a few cases (less than 10 times)
37	I have had to use some sick leave but flexitime hasn't helped me
6	I haven't had to take any sick leave

During the experiment year did you use less sick leave in total *because* flexitime has allowed you to vary your scheduled start times?

5	Yes, I've been able to save more than 10 hours sick leave
34	Yes, I've saved from 1 to 10 hours sick leave
42	No, flexitime did not help my sick leave usage
6	No, I didn't use any sick leave

Another anticipated advantage of flexitime in OMCS (Office of Management and Computer Sciences) was that there would be increased computer time available to OMCS personnel in the nonpeak hours. In your opinion:

6	Access has increased in both the A.M. and P.M. hours
6	Access has increased only in the A.M. hours
11	Access has increased only in the P.M. hours
18	Access has remained unchanged
44	No opinion or don't interface with the computer
2	No answer or doesn't know

How has the "office coverage" requirement in OMCS affected your flexitime freedom?

68	It has had no effect on me personally
13	I have had to occasionally adjust my flexitime schedule to honor office coverage
2	I frequently have to adjust my schedule to insure office coverage
4	I was unaware that we had an office coverage requirement

In your opinion, does the nature of the work in your office require the presence of a supervisor?

14	Yes, a supervisor should be present during the entire time that all of the employees are present
72	No, a supervisor need not be present during the entire time that all employees are present
1	No opinion

Are you ever asked by your supervisor to work other than your scheduled hours?

68	Rarely or never
17	Occasionally
	Frequently
2	No opinion

Do you ever feel that you must adjust your work schedule because of unusual or unanticipated job requirements or demands?

49	Rarely or never
37	Occasionally
1	Frequently

Do you think flexitime has had any effect on the productivity of your office?

40	Yes, productivity has increased
26	No, productivity has remained about the same
	Yes, productivity has decreased
21	No opinion or don't know

In your opinion has OMCS employee morale increased since flexitime?

39	Yes, I think flexitime has had a substantial positive effect on employee morale
32	Yes, I think morale has increased somewhat
16	No, I think morale has remained about the same
	No, flexitime has had a negative effect on morale

Before flexitime, how would you rate your overall job satisfaction?

8	Very high
31	High
37	Moderate
7	Low
2	Very low
2	No response

44 SECTION 1—TECHNIQUES

How do you rate your job satisfaction since flexitime?

16	Very high
36	High
27	Moderate
4	Low
2	Very low
2	No response

Do you feel that OMCS is a better place or a worse place to work as a result of flexitime?

64	A better place to work
	A worse place to work
21	Flexitime has had no effect on the work environment
2	No answer or don't know

What would you say has been the most significant disadvantage of flexitime in OMCS?

5	Nonavailability of supervisors or employees during part of the work day
3	Providing office coverage outside of the core time
1	Flexitime is not entirely compatible with our work environment
8	Timekeeping chores have increased substantially
14	Abuse of the use of flexitime
56	I'm not aware of any problems or disadvantages of flexitime in OMCS
	Other (Please explain in remarks)

How do you feel about the OMCS flexitime experiment overall?

34	Very successful
45	Successful
3	Only partially successful
	Unsuccessful
5	No opinion

Summary of suggested changes

Do away with scheduled start times	40%
Shorten core time	30%
Crack down on flexitime abuse	15%
4-day work week	5%
Flexilunch	5%
Miscellaneous	5%

The nature of some organizations does not permit flexitime. The majority of businesses and agencies, however, could well use it in one form or another to great advantage. The concept needs to be tailor made to the organization's needs and problems. A 3-month experiment in your organization may prove more problems are solved than made and that productivity is higher through flexitime.

CHAPTER 7
HOW TO HELP INDIVIDUAL STAFF MEMBERS WITH THEIR TIME MANAGEMENT

Most managers are painfully aware how poorly some staff members organize their time. Complaining doesn't help the situation and even being a good example captivates the attention of only a few. For the manager to see results he or she should pay closer attention to the staff's work habits and to be assertive in challenging them into change. Here are some suggestions:

1. *Take time to sit down and share your practices with a staff member who could benefit from your ways.* For example, an employee jumps from one job to another frequently and forgets some important items every other week. The employee obviously needs a list and a system of setting priorities. Sit down and show him or her what you do each day and indicate how it would help. Do it graciously, not accusingly. When your staff realize you are "for" them rather than "against" them, then they consider suggestions as helpful.

2. *Use 10 minutes each month at a staff meeting to let any person share any way of working that would be more productive.* Put "time-saving ideas" on the agenda and encourage the staff to come with their ideas. Some of the best observations and suggestions come from clerk-typists and secretaries.

3. *Important questions directed at staff members frequently* are "How do I interrupt your time schedule? What could I do differently that would help you do your job quicker? Is there anything I haven't delegated to you that is holding you back from completing a job?"

Managers who are open to staff members in this way tend to gain respect. Besides, when the manager wants to make a suggestion to the staff he or she has made the task easier by first being open for their feedback.

4. *Let staff members participate in deadlines as much as possible.* A major cause of frustration and resentment among staff members comes about when notes arrive on their desks reading something like "Please send following information to me by May 25th." It is already May 24 and the employee is already buried in work.

HOW TO HELP INDIVIDUAL STAFF MEMBERS WITH THEIR TIME MANAGEMENT

The employee has not been consulted as to the feasibility of giving this information by this date. This kind of communication can often be replaced by the manager or secretary phoning the employee and saying "John, I would like this information quickly. When can you have it in my hands?" If John says May 26 and the manager needs it by May 25, then the manager can say "Okay, that's one day too late, so delay the Johnson report you are working on." Proper communication and consideration makes for a more relaxed employee and therefore a more productive one. The employee is more likely to meet the deadline this way and if not, he or she is then accountable.

5. *Give appropriate recognition when you see any improvement in a staff member's management of time.* The manager who does not recognize improvements in the staff is missing the best motivation tool available. First, you should observe your staff closely and give positive as well as negative evaluation of the subordinate's performance. For example, a clerk-typist increases his or her speed from 50 to 60 words per minute in a month. He or she also makes less errors. For this to go unnoticed by the manager is almost unforgivable! You need to tell this employee that you notice the difference and that you are very pleased. That may be worth more than a pay increase and he or she will continue to improve. People like and need recognition—including you, the manager.

6. *Send staff members to a good time management workshop.* These workshops are very popular at present and are given by most management schools throughout the country.

Think of the people you work with and ask yourself how you could help each of them with his or her time scheduling. Would a quiet time help all of them? Would giving a report at the staff meeting create interest? Is there one individual in particular who could use one of the ideas in this course? Could you share the idea with him/her? While it's fresh in your mind jot down the names and ideas below and then refer to this page when you arrive back at the office.

SECTION 1—TECHNIQUES

PERSON/MEETING	SUGGESTION I WOULD LIKE TO MAKE

CHAPTER 8

HOW YOUR TOTAL OFFICE/COMPANY CAN INCREASE PRODUCTIVITY BY 10 TO 30%

Several weeks after being in one of my workshops a manager exclaimed, "I went back to my office enthused about the Q.T., priority setting conference, how to rearrange the phone system, plus other ideas, and do you know what? When I reported this at the staff meeting I was met with "that sounds good—maybe we'll look into that sometime." He is not alone. When managers attend workshops on time management, problem solving, communication skills, and a variety of other general management subjects they normally go alone from their offices. This means that for two or three days they, emotionally as well as intellectually, really understand how their offices could function much better. When they report on their findings, they discover they are alone in their enthusiasm for the concepts. The other managers may be in tune intellectually but not emotionally—they have not just spent two days in a workshop as they have.

If you are serious about your whole office doing more essential work in less time, then you can do it. The best way is to close your office at least one whole day to make everyone available from secretary to top manager for a special time management workshop. Another office or a skeleton staff from elsewhere can answer the calls that day. The best place to meet is in a hotel away from your premises. With the aid of a competent time management specialist, your whole office receives instruction on basic time management principles for individuals, and for groups working together. Everyone hears the same material. Everyone is taking time to understand it emotionally. The whole office gets the feel together of how things could be different. After the instruction is over and questions are answered, people within the office who work closely together meet with each other to apply these ideas to their situation. Each such "minigroup" then reports their findings to the whole group. The whole group then intensively discusses ways of performing in which the total staff will be able to participate. At the end of such a day most people have about five items they want to change and the whole office makes from three to six significant changes in how it will operate in the future. Not only does productivity increase, people really feel part of the whole operation. Younger staff members express appreciation for being heard. Morale is boosted.

You have the kind of operation that could not close for a whole day? What about two half days, or evenings? There's always a way.

At the end of this chapter you will find a report by an organization in Arizona that arranged to have all of its state, district, and local offices available for time management training together. Some weeks after the training, one of the supervisors said "It's a different place. I got so much work done this morning I can hardly believe it. During the office two hours of blocking interruptions, I was only disturbed twice—compared with every 5 minutes before."

By this corporate training will you increase productivity in your office by as much as 30%? That depends on the present level of effectiveness of your organization. It also depends on how much is implemented from the workshop. Such a venture, however, will be rewarded. Your office effectiveness and productivity will increase without question!

A SUCCESSFUL EXPERIMENT IN TIME MANAGEMENT

A special report compiled by Andrew Mayberry, State Director, Farmers Home Administration (Department of Agriculture) and Jim Davidson, President, People in Business.

Early in 1977 a request was made by the Arizona State Office of Farmers Home Administration (Agriculture) for a series of time management workshops to be conducted for all F.H.A. employees throughout the state. The national office in Washington agreed and training was arranged for late May and early June. The main problem throughout the state is the continuous increase in establishing new loans in addition to servicing existing loans. The main complaint was that there were not enough hours in the day to accomplish the work. The task of the workshops was to help staff members organize individual time more effectively and to help people working along side one another to work as teams, finding new ways to cooperate with each other, so that jobs would be accomplished quicker and with greater quality.

The training necessitated everyone from the same office taking the same training at the same time, regardless of grade level. In addition to the state office there are 3 district offices and 25 county offices. Some offices are very small with only two people working together, so in some of the workshops several offices were grouped together. A maximum of 25 attended each workshop. Each workshop lasted two days, each held in Phoenix.

During the two days the following subjects were considered:

1. Goals and Priorities—Both the individuals' and the organization's.
2. Weekly and Daily Planning—What items to include and what to block out in a busy work schedule.
3. Establishing High Productivity Hours—Each person determined his/her daily time period(s) when alertness was greatest. This is to assist in planning items in this period that demand concentration.
4. Blocking Interruptions—Particularly during most people's high productivity hours. Interruptions were considered in the light of the abuses brought about through the "open door" and "open space" practices.
5. Establishing an Office/Statewide Quiet Period—This was one of the highlights of the workshops—people working to agree to only crisis interruptions during certain hours of the day.
6. Reducing the Time Element in Meetings—Particular emphasis was given the agenda system and time limiting each meeting.
7. Various Time Management Techniques—Presentation of a variety of time-saving ideas.
8. Communicating with Each Other—An important aspect of time management is that the teamwork aspect of it only happens when there is a positive work atmosphere. Time was taken in the workshop to consider the kind of communicating which makes it all happen.

During the last part of the training, people working with each other formed into groups to develop a corporate action plan. Each office group determined what was workable and what was not workable in their particular situation.

After all the training was completed, representatives from all offices gathered together with the state director to determine what policy could be implemented throughout the state. The following resulted:

1. During the hours of 9:00 A.M. to 11:00 A.M. agreement was made not to contact each other unless an emergency arose. This would enable people in the offices throughout the state to organize their work at 8:00 A.M. and make necessary phone calls before 9:00 A.M. Each office had agreed on a time period when they would not bother each other internally. This corresponded to the same time period when the offices agreed not to phone each other.

2. Statewide meetings normally lasting 1 day to 1½ days a month would be accomplished in ½ day. This reduction in time would come about by having reports written beforehand and circulated, an agenda for each meeting, and only concentrating on high priority items within a fixed time limit.

It is not possible in this report to indicate the impact that was made on each participant and it would be laborious to report on each separate office's specific action plans, but below are a number of important results from the whole operation.

1. Individuals practicing preworkday planning and priority setting. Self-organization.
2. Staff meetings, and most other meetings and conferences are being conducted in the afternoons using the agenda system, prepared handouts, time limits on items, and minutes to enable follow-up decisions. Only staff members needed for that particular staff meeting are required to be in attendance.

3. Establishment of a 1- or 2-hour period in the morning when staff members will allow each other to do his/her concentration-type work free from unnecessary interruptions. For many people this has resulted in as much as a 30% increase in productivity.
4. Physical layout changes, for example, closing a door, changing desks, relocating coffee pot or photocopying machine.
5. Increase in morale. The training and subsequent change in operations has had the effect of a greater sense of accomplishment.
6. Development of team cooperation. Training taken together had the effect of greater understanding between individuals working with each other plus separate offices having contact with each other.
7. Mutual support. Because of consciousness of each other's problems and implementation of mutual policies, if a customer should make a complaint to the state director about an employee's treatment of that customer in a county office, and that treatment was due to agreed policy, the state director is able to support the county office employee where appropriate.
8. Reeducating the public. Encouraging visits by appointment and during specified hours.

Other interesting observations from the whole operation are that:

* Some of the keenest insights and suggestions came from secretaries and clerk-typists!
* The training would not have been successful if people had not taken it together as an office unit—about 90% voiced this opinion.
* The cost was minimal and small compared with other forms of training for so many people.
* Participants indicated that the operation was considered to be highly successful and in most instances the training was considered the most practical and useful that they had experienced.

HOW YOUR TOTAL OFFICE/COMPANY CAN INCREASE PRODUCTIVITY 53

What do you suppose would happen if your office staff, or even part of it, attended a day (or two- or three-day) workshop together?

	CHECK THE APPROPRIATE BOX		
ON THE POSITIVE SIDE	HIGH PROBABILITY	PROBABILITY	LOW PROBABILITY
The staff in general would favor this idea.			
Consciousness level of need to save time would be raised.			
A quiet period would result in some form.			
Greater coordination would take place.			
Length of meetings would be reduced.			
Priority setting conferences would be started.			
Interruptions would be reduced.			
Other offices would be impressed.			
Some people would start to plan better.			
Morale would be increased.			
We would get rid of some Deuce items.			
Productivity would increase at least 10%.			
If it was successful, it would help me personally.			

	CHECK THE APPROPRIATE BOX		
ON THE NEGATIVE SIDE	HIGH PROBABILITY	PROBABILITY	LOW PROBABILITY
Top management would be hard to convince.			
Some people would find it threatening.			
If it was not successful, I would be blamed.			

40 WAYS TO SAVE TIME

Following is a summary of ideas contained in the previous chapters plus other easy-to-use techniques.

1. Write down your ideas. Do not trust your memory however good it might be!
2. Set your priorities first thing in the morning before any work gets underway.
3. Have a priority-setting meeting early in the day.
4. Use your high productivity hours for your Ace and King (Jack) projects.
5. Do not overschedule. Leave two hours of the day free from appointments.
6. Tackle time-consuming projects in stages.
7. Delegate to your staff the items that they are capable of doing.
8. Teach your staff how to perform certain tasks so that you can delegate in the future.
9. Concentrate on one item at a time.
10. Institute a quiet period in your office, preferably in the morning.
11. When a day's work is taxing, get out of the office at lunchtime. Plan to have lunch with a friend or do something recreational.
12. Have a light lunch and little or no alcohol at lunchtime. This prevents the usually "sleepy" period between 1:00 P.M. and 2:00 P.M.
13. Use your low productivity hour(s) for easy-to-do projects and casual reading.
14. Work on the appointment system as much as possible.
15. Have the secretary screen phone calls and inform him or her when you do not wish to be disturbed.
16. Have your secretary situated between you and visitors.
17. Close the door when you don't want to be disturbed. Use a high movable partition around you if you don't have a private office.
18. Meet visitors outside your office and talk with them standing if you wish the consultation to be brief.
19. Time limit visits. When someone calls for an appointment ask how long the consultation will be.
20. Carry a 3 X 5 card to jot down ideas when you are away from your desk.
21. Carry reading material with you at all times. Use waiting time to read.
22. Dictate letters and reports. Use the dictaphone.
23. Keep letters brief. Only address the issue. Do not say more than is required.
24. Use travel time to listen to important material contained on tapes.
25. Have a place for everything.
26. Keep your desk free of papers you are not working on that day. This prevents papers being mixed up or lost.
27. Set reasonable deadlines for yourself and others.

28. Make decisions now if possible. If further information is not likely to change the course of the decision, then don't wait any longer.
29. Keep paperwork moving.
30. Mark what you read with pencil. When you have to refer to that document later you will not have to read it all again.
31. If something isn't clear ask for clarification. Do not assume. You might find you have to do it all over again.
32. Use 10 minutes of staff meetings once a month to exchange time-saving ideas.
33. Put meetings and consultations to the afternoon, preferably 1½ hours before quitting time. Put meetings in the morning only if they demand maximum concentration from all the members.
34. Use the agenda system for meetings.
35. Keep meetings to an hour or less.
36. Form an ad hoc committee in meetings for items that need more investigation. Do not take up people's time talking about an item that nobody can adequately address.
37. Have short meetings in a room with no chairs. Keep standing.
38. Close your office, or part of it, for one day to have a time management workshop where all levels participate.
39. Where you work closely with another person, collect items and talk with him or her at certain times. Do not make contact every time you have an item. Encourage others to do the same.
40. Investigate the feasibility of using flexitime.

DAILY WORKSHEET/TIME SCHEDULE

ITEMS TO DO		EARLY MORNING
		8:00
		8:15
		8:30
		8:45
		9:00
		9:15
		9:30
		9:45
		10:00
		10:15
		10:30
		10:45
		11:00
		11:15
		11:30
		11:45
	DELEGATE TO	
A ♣		12:00
		12:15
		12:30
		12:45
		1:00
		1:15
		1:30
		1:45
K ♣		
		2:00
		2:15
		2:30
		2:45
		3:00
		3:15
		3:30
		3:45
J ♣		
		4:00
		4:15
		4:30
		4:45
		5:00
		LATE AFTERNOON
2 ♣		

DAILY WORKSHEET/TIME SCHEDULE

ITEMS TO DO		EARLY MORNING
		8:00
		8:15
		8:30
		8:45
		9:00
		9:15
		9:30
		9:45
		10:00
		10:15
		10:30
		10:45
		11:00
		11:15
		11:30
		11:45
	DELEGATE TO	
		12:00
A♣		12:15
		12:30
		12:45
		1:00
		1:15
		1:30
		1:45
K♣		
		2:00
		2:15
		2:30
		2:45
		3:00
		3:15
		3:30
		3:45
J♣		
		4:00
		4:15
		4:30
		4:45
		5:00
		LATE AFTERNOON
2♣		

DAILY WORKSHEET/TIME SCHEDULE

ITEMS TO DO		EARLY MORNING
		8:00
		8:15
		8:30
		8:45
		9:00
		9:15
		9:30
		9:45
		10:00
		10:15
		10:30
		10:45
		11:00
		11:15
		11:30
		11:45
	DELEGATE TO	
A♣		12:00
		12:15
		12:30
		12:45
		1:00
		1:15
		1:30
		1:45
K♣		2:00
		2:15
		2:30
		2:45
		3:00
		3:15
		3:30
		3:45
J♣		4:00
		4:15
		4:30
		4:45
		5:00
		LATE AFTERNOON
2♣		

DAILY WORKSHEET/TIME SCHEDULE

ITEMS TO DO		DELEGATE TO	EARLY MORNING
			8:00
			8:15
			8:30
			8:45
			9:00
			9:15
			9:30
			9:45
			10:00
			10:15
			10:30
			10:45
			11:00
			11:15
			11:30
			11:45
A♣			12:00
			12:15
			12:30
			12:45
			1:00
			1:15
			1:30
			1:45
K♣			
			2:00
			2:15
			2:30
			2:45
			3:00
			3:15
			3:30
			3:45
J♣			
			4:00
			4:15
			4:30
			4:45
			5:00
2♣			**LATE AFTERNOON**

DAILY WORKSHEET/TIME SCHEDULE

ITEMS TO DO		EARLY MORNING
		8:00
		8:15
		8:30
		8:45
		9:00
		9:15
		9:30
		9:45
		10:00
		10:15
		10:30
		10:45
		11:00
		11:15
		11:30
		11:45
	DELEGATE TO	
		12:00
A ♣		12:15
		12:30
		12:45
		1:00
		1:15
		1:30
		1:45
K ♣		
		2:00
		2:15
		2:30
		2:45
		3:00
		3:15
		3:30
		3:45
J ♣		
		4:00
		4:15
		4:30
		4:45
		5:00
2 ♣		**LATE AFTERNOON**

DAILY WORKSHEET/TIME SCHEDULE

ITEMS TO DO		EARLY MORNING
		8:00
		8:15
		8:30
		8:45
		9:00
		9:15
		9:30
		9:45
		10:00
		10:15
		10:30
		10:45
		11:00
		11:15
		11:30
		11:45
	DELEGATE TO	
A ♣		12:00
		12:15
		12:30
		12:45
		1:00
		1:15
		1:30
		1:45
K ♣		
		2:00
		2:15
		2:30
		2:45
		3:00
		3:15
		3:30
		3:45
J ♣		
		4:00
		4:15
		4:30
		4:45
		5:00
		LATE AFTERNOON
2 ♣		

DAILY WORKSHEET/TIME SCHEDULE

ITEMS TO DO		EARLY MORNING
		8:00
		8:15
		8:30
		8:45
		9:00
		9:15
		9:30
		9:45
		10:00
		10:15
		10:30
		10:45
		11:00
		11:15
		11:30
		11:45
	DELEGATE TO	
		12:00
A♣		12:15
		12:30
		12:45
		1:00
		1:15
		1:30
		1:45
K♣		2:00
		2:15
		2:30
		2:45
		3:00
		3:15
		3:30
		3:45
J♣		4:00
		4:15
		4:30
		4:45
		5:00
		LATE AFTERNOON
2♣		

HOW YOUR TOTAL OFFICE/COMPANY CAN INCREASE PRODUCTIVITY 63

DAILY WORKSHEET/TIME SCHEDULE

ITEMS TO DO		EARLY MORNING
		8:00
		8:15
		8:30
		8:45
		9:00
		9:15
		9:30
		9:45
		10:00
		10:15
		10:30
		10:45
		11:00
		11:15
		11:30
		11:45
	DELEGATE TO	
		12:00
A♣		12:15
		12:30
		12:45
		1:00
		1:15
		1:30
		1:45
K♣		
		2:00
		2:15
		2:30
		2:45
		3:00
		3:15
		3:30
		3:45
J♣		
		4:00
		4:15
		4:30
		4:45
		5:00
		LATE AFTERNOON
2♣		

DAILY WORKSHEET/TIME SCHEDULE

ITEMS TO DO		EARLY MORNING
		8:00
		8:15
		8:30
		8:45
		9:00
		9:15
		9:30
		9:45
		10:00
		10:15
		10:30
		10:45
		11:00
		11:15
		11:30
		11:45
	DELEGATE TO	
		12:00
A♣		12:15
		12:30
		12:45
		1:00
		1:15
		1:30
		1:45
K♣		
		2:00
		2:15
		2:30
		2:45
		3:00
		3:15
		3:30
		3:45
J♣		
		4:00
		4:15
		4:30
		4:45
		5:00
2♣		
		LATE AFTERNOON

DAILY WORKSHEET/TIME SCHEDULE

ITEMS TO DO		EARLY MORNING
		8:00
		8:15
		8:30
		8:45
		9:00
		9:15
		9:30
		9:45
		10:00
		10:15
		10:30
		10:45
		11:00
		11:15
		11:30
	DELEGATE TO	11:45
A ♣		12:00
		12:15
		12:30
		12:45
		1:00
		1:15
		1:30
		1:45
K ♣		
		2:00
		2:15
		2:30
		2:45
		3:00
		3:15
		3:30
		3:45
J ♣		
		4:00
		4:15
		4:30
		4:45
		5:00
2 ♣		
		LATE AFTERNOON

SECTION 2 BEHAVIOR

CHAPTER 9
WHY PEOPLE MISMANAGE TIME

The question is not "Do I mismanage my time?" but rather, "How much of my time do I waste needlessly?" because it appears that all of us mismanage time somewhere in the working day. The *degree* to which we mismanage time varies greatly.

Here are six categories of people that tend to waste an inordinate amount of time.

1. The recognition seeker is the worker who looks and acts harried. He or she often dashes around the office, has his or her desk piled with work, sits back and says, "Wow, this is some task, isn't it?" in the presence of the staff. The recognition seeker wants them to recognize how busy he or she is and that if it weren't for him or her the whole office might fall apart. The recognition seeker fails to plan carefully, for if that happened he or she would have no reason to rush around. Then the staff wouldn't give the desired recognition that goes like, "My, you shouldn't do so much."

Another kind of recognition seeker is the employee who talks incessantly. This person looks for a captive audience—the switchboard operator or 20 people seated in a staff meeting where he or she is heard more than anyone else. This individual has a great need to be heard and so takes twice as long as normal to explain a matter.

2. The complainer wastes time by blaming the organizational structure or people in the office for most things that happen. He or she then excuses him or herself for not making decisions and accomplishing the work. The complainer makes a heavy atmosphere for other workers and usually finds someone who will listen. The complainer wastes time harping about how matters should be instead of recognizing how they really are and then making constructive moves to make things better.

3. The "I'll Show You" person acts a great deal out of resentment and blocks constructive work from proceeding swiftly.

Case: John and Mary worked in the same section with each other for 2 years. A vacancy then occurred for which they both applied. Mary was chosen for the position. John congratulated her, but felt he was more qualified for the job. Some time later, Mary had occasion to phone John to receive a report from him. John promised to send it to her in two days. Nothing happened. Mary phoned after 3 days—"John, do you have that report?"

"Well Mary, I haven't got all the information and things are so busy here. I need some statistics from Janice but she is out today."

"My boss is screaming at me, John, for not having the report."

"Well I understand your position, Mary, and I'll try to have it by tomorrow, but I'm not Superman, you know."

In reality John could have sent the report the day after Mary initially asked him, but he found "legitimate" reasons why it could not be sent. His resentment got the better of him. Time was wasted for both him and Mary.

People failing to deal with their resentment in business is a major cause of mismanagement of time. It takes all kinds of subtle forms.

4. The spontaneity-loving manager says, "If I structure my day and plan carefully then I'll become a robot. I like my freedom to do what comes naturally." This person imagines that planning and saving time has a lot to do with rigidity, and it is true that many managers and salespeople do become rigid with overplanning. Effective time management leaves plenty of room for spontaneity. However, where there is no or little structure or boundary setting, there is really little or no freedom. Spontaneity-loving managers become casual. Deadlines are relaxed and employees receive confused directives.

5. The fear-ridden staff member wastes time by failing to make decisions and by not giving clear instructions. This is the person who is indecisive and indefinite by constantly asking questions like, "Are you sure this is what you want?" and by saying to a subordinate, "I'm not sure, maybe you could try it that way." He or she is hesitant and is afraid of anything backfiring. Being blamed is avoided constantly. Consequently, decisions that could be made in 5 minutes take 2 days. The important element of risk is absent.

6. The "I-Don't-Care" employee is bored with the job. He or she finds little in his or her work that is challenging or likable. This employee feels like a round peg in a square hole. He or she has lost interest and can say only, "Well, it's a job for which I get paid." The I-don't-care employee works slowly, not caring much if deadlines are not met. It is not likely he or she will aspire to top level management but this kind of person surprisingly often holds a fairly important position.

All of the above descriptions of people who waste time have one thing in common and that is that they feel they are *victims.*

*The recognition seeker feels a victim of his or her own need to have recognition.

*The complainer and I'll-Show-You persons feel victimized by the company or individuals within the company.

*The spontaneity-loving person experiences the victim feeling because of lack of control.

*The fear-ridden employee feels he or she will become a victim if he or she makes a wrong move.

*The I-Don't-Care person feels that he or she is a victim at the hands of society, that he or she is stuck, and that that's just the way it is.

Victims are losers and to be a winner you need to be in control of what you do with your time and your life. Most people are not winners all the time and most people are not losers all the time. It's all a question of degree. Below are two sets of boxes—one representing winning and the other representing losing. In Figure 1, the shaded part shows that the "winner" operates in the winning box most of the time, but now and again feels like a loser and plays that role.

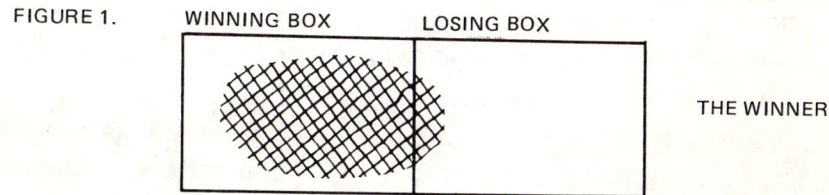

In Figure 2, the shaded part shows that the "loser" operates in the losing box most of the time, but now and again feels like a winner.

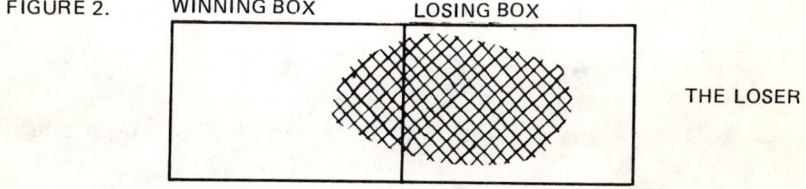

Figure 3 indicates a mixture. This person has lots of ups and downs. He or she oscillates a great deal.

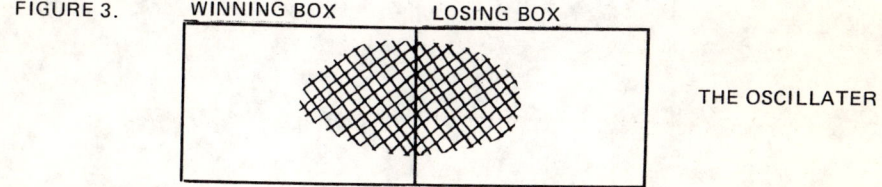

Nobody really wants to be a loser

People who settle for being victims and losers do so because they *feel* they are not capable of being in control of themselves and winning. How then can a manager or salesperson reduce or eliminate being a victim? How can he or she become more constructive, spending time positively and creatively? How can a manager or salesperson stop being a complainer or reduce the time taken in seeking recognition? There is no simple answer to these questions but below are six steps that will help you identify problem areas and lead you to winning concrete decisions. To give you a better idea of how to respond to the steps, notes made by John, a salesman for an interior designing company, are in the right-hand column.

STEP 1. *IDENTIFY IN YOUR JOB THINGS YOU HAVE DONE DURING THE PAST 6 MONTHS THAT MAKE YOU FEEL LIKE A "WINNER"*

> Made about 100 new contacts.
> Clinched the "Munroe" order.
> Suggested three new marketing techniques to boss that were implemented.
> Increased sales by 10% over previous 6 months.

STEP 2. *IDENTIFY IN YOUR JOB THINGS YOU HAVE DONE/OR NOT DONE DURING THE PAST 6 MONTHS THAT MAKE YOU FEEL LIKE A "LOSER"*

> Still have a poor relationship with boss.
> Lost the ILB account.
> Not seeing enough people in day.
> Not making as much money as desired.
> Not making a decision to stay in job or look elsewhere.

WHY PEOPLE MISMANAGE TIME   73

STEP 3. *BELOW ARE SIX KINDS OF PEOPLE THAT MISMANAGE TIME. CHECK THE ONE YOU IDENTIFY WITH MORE THAN ANY OF THE OTHER FIVE. IF YOU DO NOT IDENTIFY WITH ANY OF THE SIX, WRITE IN YOUR DESCRIPTION OF THE KIND OF PERSON YOU MOST IDENTIFY WITH ON THE "OTHER" LINE*

Recognition seeker	
Complainer	
"I'll show you"	
Spontaneity loving	Spontaneity loving
Fear ridden	(I hate sitting down to plan!)
"I don't care"	
(other)	

STEP 4. *IF YOU WERE TO COMPARE YOUR ORGANIZATION TO A SPORTING EVENT, WHAT WOULD IT BE? WHAT PART WOULD YOU BE PLAYING, IF ANY?*

> Golf. You can play it by yourself. We don't work as a team! I feel on my own too much. Not enough support. I'm playing on my green and everyone else is on his or her own green.

STEP 5. *ALLOW STEPS 2, 3, AND 4 TO RAISE YOUR LEVEL OF AWARENESS OF NEGATIVE ASPECTS ABOUT YOURSELF AND YOUR ORGANIZATION. NOW DESCRIBE HOW YOU WOULD LIKE IT TO BE OTHERWISE.*

> Better planning.
> Better relationship with boss.
> More give and take interaction.
> Increase in sales.

74 SECTION 2—BEHAVIOR

STEP 6. *NOW LIST ANY AND ALL CONCRETE "DOABLE" THINGS THAT YOU MIGHT POSSIBLY ENGAGE IN TO BRING ABOUT DESIRED CHANGE IN YOURSELF AND OTHERS. WHEN YOU HAVE MADE THE LIST CHECK THE ITEMS THAT LOOK THE MOST LIKELY TO BE EFFECTIVE.*

> Make out a weekly schedule.
> Market in geographical locations.
> Service old accounts in Georgetown area.
> Shoot the boss.
> Tell the boss more of what I want from him or her.
> Suggest a sales techniques hour once a month.
> Take time to write notes immediately.
> Make inquiries re other work—talk with Allen.

Managing the day more effectively often means change. Even minor changes can turn out to be significant. Whenever changes are made, two elements are essential. One is *honesty* and the other is *desire*. To be in control of your times means being honest about your own strengths and weaknesses in how you operate. It also takes desire to make things better. Changes take place when you want them to happen. They rarely take place because you say they "should."

Now that you have worked through these six steps, you have made yourself aware of items that you can do to help with the management of your day. You will put them into operation soon—if you want.

CHAPTER 10

HOW TO COUNTERACT PROCRASTINATION

"Procrastination is the thief of time" is an old saying that has enough support from real life to make it valid in 9 cases out of 10. Procrastination happens so often that it appears there are powerful forces behind it. People do not stop procrastinating simply through being preached at with injunctions like "Do it now!" Most of us realize that we ought not to put things off but we do, despite feelings of guilt or frustrations.

Exactly what do we mean by procrastination? It is the act (passive or active) of putting off to a later date what appears needful to be done now or very soon. Putting jobs off until next week may not be procrastinating if these jobs could legitimately wait until then. Procrastination has the essential element of putting off what should be done today.

Procrastination has its roots in childhood

(You didn't start procrastinating the day you started that job that you don't like!) Children are in touch with what they want and what they don't want, more so than adults. Children will perform a house duty shoddily or not at all or two weeks later *if they sense they can get away with it*. Procrastination becomes a fairly accepted form of behavior for some people simply because they were allowed to put things off. This forms the habit. But in the work situation, employees will find themselves in plenty of trouble by putting off items they think unpleasant. They must kick the habit or go elsewhere, only to discover their procrastinating rarely goes in their favor.

If you are a procrastinator (most of us are, to one degree or another) consider the following steps to help you reduce or even eliminate your procrastination.

Identify the tasks in your business that you are leaving undone, doing inadequately, or putting off. Make a list and be specific. You could also do this for tasks outside of work. You will see at a glance that for one reason or another you really don't want to do these tasks.

Ask yourself the question, "Why don't I want to do this job?" Ask the same question for each item. For example, a manager keeps putting off going through his piled up in-basket because he really dislikes paperwork. He prefers being in meetings and talking with people. Or, the boss has told an employee to make an analysis of a project. The employee thinks the project is hopeless and feels it is a waste of time to make the analysis, so he or she delays as much as possible—as long as the boss permits the delay.

Ask yourself another question, "Since I don't enjoy this task, is it possible for me to give it to someone else to do, particularly someone who might enjoy doing it?" Don't answer that question with a "no" too quickly. We often feel stuck with tasks, but a little exploring might help us to discover that it might be delegated to someone else.

Taking the examples above, the manager may find that the secretary could deal with most items in the "in-basket" and may find it interesting—a break from the typing. Or, the employee who is ordered to make the analysis may find someone who believes in the project and would like to do the job. A word with the boss may make the transference easier. Since the tasks we do well are generally the ones we like doing, it makes sense to move work around in the office so that more people are working projects that are desired. This is not always possible and there are limits. For example, a sales manager may enjoy calling on certain customers. His or her time is so utilized in selling that his or her managerial function is neglected. That would be problematic. But as a general rule, within limits, go after the tasks you like performing and delegate the others, if that delegation is legitimate. This helps us to counteract depression or anxiety caused by too many tasks that are not desired.

Now if you can't delegate the task or it would cause problems if you did, and you really need to do it:

Ask yourself a third question, "What happens to me when I procrastinate with that job?" What happens to me is usually negative. For example, an executive keeps putting off having a meeting with some staff members. Each time he or she is asked about the meeting the executive gets upset and inwardly feels guilty. He or she can rationalize why not to have the meeting now yet knows "deep-down" that it is necessary. What happens is that the executive becomes *upset* and *feels guilty*. In transactional analysis this is called the "negative payoff." Another example would be an employee who procrastinates with his or her report. The employee rarely has it ready on time. He or she is scolded by the manager and consequently feels "kicked." The employee can then complain to other employees, "I know I was late with the report, but there is no reason in the world why he should scold me or any other human being like that. After all, we all are late with project now and again." The negative payoff is complaining and perhaps eventually *conflict* with the boss. Look for the feeling that results from procrastinating. It is negative and destructive.

These feelings include guilt, frustration, depression, anxiety, conflict, and rebellion, which can then lead to other negatives.

Are the negatives that come from procrastinating really worth it to you personally? What good is your negative payoff to you? In becoming aware of the real negatives that come to you through procrastinating, you are in a good position to see why you might want to give up the practice of putting things off. It just isn't worth it!

You can acknowledge you don't want to do the job, yet you have the power to decide to do it. It's acceptable to not want to perform certain tasks. Some things we like to do and others we don't like to do. That's natural. A salesperson may not like to call on a certain customer. He or she can't delegate the task to someone else. He or she doesn't want to lose the account and sees it would be beneficial to make the call. Procrastination makes the salesperson feel guilty about not doing his or her job properly. He or she should now control him or herself and make a decision to go and see the customer—because really it's in the salesperson's best interest to do so.

There is a world of difference between feeling that you "have" to do it and "deciding" to do it. "Having" to do a job means you are being controlled. "Deciding" to do it means you are in control.

Case: Johnson is a GS-9 working for the federal government. He is a new supervisor and enjoys directing and controlling the few people he supervises. His boss is a GS-14 who requires him to make out lengthy reports and directs him to tasks that take him away from the function of supervising. Johnson is frustrated, holds up reports, and performs tasks for his GS-14 boss in a haphazard way. This brings him into conflict with his boss and the possibility of a poor evaluation. Johnson's payoff is conflict with his boss. Johnson is heading for an ulcer! Johnson brings the whole area under his control when he makes decisions. He decides to discuss the matter with his boss and finds his boss is insistent that Johnson spend less time with the people he is supervising and more time on his projects. Johnson resolves the conflict by deciding to go along with the boss, although he disagrees. Reports are done on time now. He decides to talk with his staff about the less time he will spend with them on their jobs and will try to make arrangements accordingly. He also decides that he wants a good evaluation and that when he becomes a GS-14 he will act differently from his present boss. He is making decisions that bring him in control of himself. He feels better about himself now. He has no need to procrastinate and the lack of conflict with his boss gives him a calmer stomach.

You can make unpleasant tasks more palatable by breaking them up into sections and doing a little at a time. Supposing a manager is required to make up the budget for next year. The manager doesn't like this task. So, what he or she can do is sit down and analyze the budget and find out all that is required to complete the figures. This might entail (1) looking at last year's figures, (2) analyzing present rate of spending, (3) calling a budget meeting, (4) obtaining estimates from six people in the office, and so on. With careful planning the manager will not leave this item to the last day, so he or she can look at last year's figures today and decide to analyze the present rate of spending tomorrow, and so on. This process of breaking unpleasant tasks into components is descriptively called the "Swiss Cheese" method by Alan Lakein. You gradually perform the tasks by making holes in it by spending 10 minutes on it this morning and another 10 minutes on it this afternoon.

Congratulate yourself when you stop procrastinating on an item! Give yourself credit. Eliminating procrastination is a victory. It makes you a winner. If nobody else pats you on the back for it, pat yourself!

The tasks I put off, do inadequately, or don't do at all.	The reason(s) why I don't want to do it.	I could legitimately delegate it to:	The negative payoff I receive is:	The decision I'd like to make to put me in control.	How I plan to carry it out.

CHAPTER 11
WORK HABITS AND THEIR EFFECT ON TIME STRUCTURING

Throughout life we have heard many messages as to how we should think, feel, act, and talk. These messages come from parents, church, school, TV, and a host of other sources. We don't all hear the same messages with the same degree of emphasis, but we do hear, evaluate, and eventually—consciously or unconsciously—decide what to be and how to be it.

To help us put a handle on these messages, analysts in the transactional analysis (TA) movement have put them into five categories. These five strong messages that we hear are:

To be perfect
To try hard
To be pleasing
To hurry up
To be strong

Each one of them is called a "Driver" because they are forceful driving forces within our lives. The tendency is for us to identify with one of these drivers more than the others. This is the Primary Driver. The Secondary Driver is the second strongest driver within us. For example, I may discover that my primary driver is "Be Perfect." This means I am a perfectionist. Everything need to be done just right. I have a tendency to nitpick. I am critical of other people's work that is substandard in my eyes. Because my work is very thoroughly done, I rarely have anything come back to me to be reworked. In other words, my general life-style is centered in making things as perfect as possible. Of course, there are exceptions but the general rule still stands. When I am not operating in this driver I discover that my most prevalent driver is "Be Pleasing." I find I have a great need to please others so I go out of my way to make sure they get what they want, and of course, I'll employ my primary driver at that point—I'll do a perfect job for them!

All five drivers are part of our personality at one time or another so don't feel overwhelmed if you feel you identify with all of them. But, we do not identify with all five equally. In the workshop situation, 80% of the participants identify with one of these drivers in particular. It normally takes 20 minutes to explain the drivers before the participants pick out the one that is their primary driver. The other 20% discover theirs by the time the workshop is over!

When you become very familiar with the drivers (see following pages) you can be working with someone for half an hour and pick out his/her primary driver. Words, body language, and tone of voice give the clues. This is tremendously valuable because, in knowing your driver and the other person's, you sense how you will relate well and what will probably be problematic between you. Then you can work on reducing these problems (see case study on page 00).

To become familiar with the various characteristics of each driver consult the outlines on the next pages. Remember that the characteristics for each driver outlined there are generally true and that there are exceptions to the rule.

Knowing your own primary driver is extremely helpful in tracing what you spend time on both to your benefit and detriment. For example, if I am a "hurry up" kind of employee I work at projects quickly. I imagine I can do more in a day than is realistic; I talk with people speedily, rush around a good deal, and become impatient if a job has too many details. All this may mean I accomplish a great deal, but I notice certain work comes back to me for lack of detail and I have to work at it again. I also find that my quick gestures with my staff make them feel uneasy and unheard and this creates a problem. Knowing my driver helps me to be aware of my strengths and weaknesses as I manage the job. I also need to learn how to "step out" of my driver, so to speak, when it doesn't serve me or my job.

THE "BE PERFECT" DRIVER

Words and Phrases

The words make for clarity. This person doesn't want any misunderstandings, so he or she qualifies a lot and covers all bases. Sometimes this person takes great pains to do this, using such phrases as:

"Are you sure you have all the necessary instructions?"

"Well, that letter is not a hundred percent clear."

"I think that's right, but we will have to pay attention to this eventually."

"We can't go on with this project as it is. We don't have all the details yet."

"Clearly that's right and that other way is wrong."

Moralistic words characterize many perfectionists—should, ought, never, always, right, wrong.

Tones

The perfectionist doesn't "slur" when talking. His words are fairly clipped. This person often speaks in a righteous tone, making others feel insignificant or guilty. The perfectionist's critical nature can make him sound harsh.

Physical Expressions

Fairly erect and even rigid. The perfectionist may count on his fingers and uses his hands a lot to explain so that you understand clearly. If the perfectionist has little humor, he will have a stern face. The perfectionist can be quite tense.

Inner Thoughts and Feelings

The perfectionist thinks a lot about quality and chastises himself if he doesn't do a good job. The perfectionist feels that if everything is done just right, things will be O.K. He often hears a voice inside that says "You should do better." On the positive side the perfectionist may be able to accept praise from himself or others when he sees he has done an excellent job.

THE "TRY HARD" DRIVER

Words and Phrases

The "try harder" is somewhat hesitant. She's a real plodder. She works hard and her words reflect it.
"Wow, I really can't get with this today."
"Well, I'm trying to do it but it will take time."
"I'm not sure if I can but I'll do my best."
"I don't know how it will turn out but we'll work on it."

Tones

She goes through different tones depending on the state of the job. She can sound frustrated, even impatient, but she is not fast speaking (unless the secondary driver is "hurry up"). Her words are fairly deliberate. She may do a lot of sighing.

Physical Expressions

She wears a frown, looks perplexed, and is sometimes fatigued. Like in the "be perfect" driver, she can be tense if she is very conscientious. She sits forward, elbows on legs.

Inner Thoughts and Feelings

She thinks a great deal about her true ability to do the job. She keeps driving herself to try harder and if things go wrong she feels she can't be blamed for trying.

THE "PLEASE ME" DRIVER

Words and Phrases

These words reflect avoidance of conflict. This person will be as accommodating as possible and sometimes overcomplimentary of others.

"Do you think you could possibly have that for me by this afternoon?"

"Oh, that's wonderful!"

"Oh, I didn't know you wanted it typed that way. I'll do it again, I'm really sorry."

"I think it will do just fine. If there's any problem, I'm sure we can attend to it. Thanks a million."

Tones

The tone is often high, sometimes whiny. This person asks a lot of questions so the voice modulates up at the end of the sentence. It normally has a pleasant or pleasing sound.

Physical Expressions

This person is a little nervous, with smiling face, raised eyebrows, hands outstretched, and an almost constant nodding head up and down in an affirmative fashion.

Inner Thoughts and Feelings

He thinks a lot about being acceptable. He feels that putting others first is important and he will gain approval. He beats himself by telling himself he's not good enough. He is fearful of being disliked and enjoys being highly praised.

THE "HURRY UP" DRIVER

Words and Phrases

She expresses urgency and the need for speed in her words.
"Let's get going—there's no need to bother about that just now."
"Forget the details, just give me the main part of the report."
"Do you mean that's all you did this morning?"
"O.K., O.K., mail it to me next week and I'll take care of it."
"It looks like I'll have to do this myself. Otherwise it will be Christmas before he gets that order."

Tones

The voice carries an impatient tone. Speech is usually rapid. An extreme "hurry up" person sounds like a machine gun. There is a wide range of voice modulation up and down.

Physical Expressions

The "hurry up" driver moves quickly, taps fingers, sits in meetings in an impatient manner. She is always on the move and can be very nervous.

Inner Thoughts and Feelings

She thinks about time and feels she is fighting the clock constantly. She complains about there not being enough hours in the day. Feeling responsible for work being done, the "hurry up" driver becomes very frustrated if time is being wasted. She wants to finish peoples' sentences for them if they are slow at speaking. She may be able to congratulate herself for "all" she has accomplished.

THE "BE STRONG" DRIVER

Words and Phrases

She shows few emotions and is not demonstrative in speech. Words are matter of fact and often minimal. When asked a question this person would like to answer with a simple "yes" or "no."
"That will do."
"I don't have any opinion about that."
"I see."
"In my judgment it would be better to forget the whole business."

Tones

Tones are monotonous, dry, and sometimes hard. There is very little voice variation. Few emotions are expressed.

Physical Expressions

These consist of a rigid body, with arms folded and an unemotional, plastic facial look.

Inner Thoughts and Feelings

She thinks about strength and independence and is fearful of letting her feelings out. This person thinks people will take advantage of her if she gives an inch. She doesn't want to get close or involved.

Drivers can work for us or against us. You will not want to get rid of your driver if it has too many benefits. Besides, it would probably be impossible for you to destroy your primary driver, especially since it is so much a part of your whole being. What we can do, however, is to keep the positive aspects of our primary driver and reduce the negative aspects.

Case: Andrews is a middle manager. He is competent in his field as an engineer and has reached his present position because of his ability plus his accommodating nature. He realizes that his primary driver is "please me." It has worked for him in the past and he senses it works for him presently with his immediate boss who is hard to get along with, in most employees' estimation. He goes the second mile for his boss and receives praise for doing so. His staff also like him. He welcomes them into his office and spends time with them on their problems. Now he discovers the negative sides of his driver. His staff is taking so much of his time, he can't get everything done in the day so he takes work home, displeasing his wife. Also, since he is pleasing and would rarely chastise anyone, he does not insist on deadlines being met. The staff take advantage of this and it is causing him problems.

Andrews needs to concentrate on (a) limiting frequency of visits from staff members and (b) making sure deadlines are met. His task is not easy because he still wants to come out as being pleasing to his staff, but if he doesn't do something he will find himself in greater conflict than he is already. Andrews needs to be firm. If he is not he will be frustrated and eventually resentful. He needs to step out of his "please me" driver at this point. He can resolve the dilemma by calling his staff together, assure them of his listening ear, and tell them of his need to have a 2-hour period in the morning free of interruptions. He can explain the seriousness of deadlines not being met and make each person who fails accountable.

Case: Mary Brown is an executive secretary who has a distinct "hurry up" driver. She is normally very effective and she manages to cover a lot of ground in the day for which her boss is very pleased. Part of her job is to make arrangements for high-level executive meetings. People attend these meetings coming from all parts of the country. Problems have emerged because executives have not been clear about what arrangements have been made, and what haven't. Details such as arranging with the hotel manager for a sign to be put up indicating conference rooms have been omitted. Mary recognizes that her driver works for her generally, but in this instance it is working against her. She needs to take time to plan these meetings in every detail. She now needs to step into her "be perfect" driver—which she may have little patience with! Mary Brown needs to make a conscious decision like "I will allocate 3 hours to plan this meeting. I will not rush. I will go over the details again and double check them with someone else if necessary." She can keep her "hurry up" driver for most of the day, but not when she is making arrangements for these meetings.

A conscious decision to step out of your primary driver when it doesn't serve you is essential.

YOUR PRIMARY DRIVER AND TIME MANAGEMENT

Identify your primary driver and list all its advantages for you on the job.

How does your driver save you time?

List all the disadvantages of your driver.

How does your driver cost you time?

Describe how your driver affects the work habits of those working with you.

What do you think your company or agency feels about your driver?

What specific changes would you like to make so that the negative aspects coming from your driver will be reduced?

How much time do you think you would save in a week if you made these changes?

ESSENTIAL ADVANTAGES AND DISADVANTAGES OF THE DRIVERS IN RELATION TO TIME

Driver	Advantage	Disadvantage
Be perfect	Completes a task so that it will not need to be redone. Very orderly. Items can be found easily. Plans carefully.	Spending too much time doing a perfect job on projects that do not need detailed analysis. Explains more than is necessary. Can overplan, making the project longer.
Try hard	Accomplishes tasks, even if not quickly.	Does not take short cuts. Makes decisions slowly. May not take risks.
Please me	Accommodates to the needs of others. Makes for harmony. Saves time for other people.	Leaves own work in favor of others. Allows others to eat into his or her time, then rushes his or her own projects or works overtime. Desire to please everyone is time consuming. Asks too many questions and has too many consultations.
Hurry up	Does a lot of work in a short time. Is excellent on jobs that do not require detail.	Hurries through important work, missing details. Receives work to do over again. Doesn't take time with staff to explain. Staff assumes and makes mistakes costing time.
Be strong	Makes balanced rational decisions free of most emotions. Personality is such that he or she is not bothered much by staff. Is freer of interruptions than most managers.	Is poor with human relations. Usually has staff problems that eat up time for the whole office.

QUESTIONS THAT NEED TO BE ASKED

The "be perfect" person should ask:
"What am I spending time on that does not require first class performance?"

The "try hard" person should ask:
"Is it really that hard? What short cuts could I take so that it can be accomplished soon?"

The "please me" person should ask:
"What must I accomplish today even though I don't do anything for anyone else? How can I please myself as well as others?"

The "hurry up" person should ask:
"What tasks need my fullest attention? When can I plan them in the day so that I will not need to rush?"

The "be strong" person should ask:
"If I were more open with my staff what would really happen? Does my fearful fantasy have any substantial foundation?"

CHAPTER 12
ASSERTIVE BEHAVIOR AS A TIME SAVER

Assertiveness Training (A/T) courses have become extremely popular during the past three years. They started for women and minorities and are now being conducted for both sexes at all staff positions including high-level executives (which are mainly male and white). A/T lays stress on the importance of each individual in the working situation, and the need for him (or her) to go after whatever that person wants from his or her job and life, as long as he or she does not violate the rights of others. How to achieve this involves learning effective communication skills and practice at putting these skills into action. This is the task of A/T workshops.

Basically A/T teaches that there are three main forms of communication. *Agressiveness* takes place when we go after what we want, with forceful energy and initiative. In the process we sometimes violate the rights of others. This means we act toward others as if they were less important human beings. An extreme aggressive act (bordering on hostility) would be one person pushing another off the sidewalk while saying "Get out of my way." A milder aggressive act would be saying to your secretary "The way you typed that letter isn't very good, is it?" This kind of communication puts people down and whether the form is extreme or mild, resentment and friction result. In the business setting it results in noncooperation, which ultimately means terrific time loss. *Nonassertiveness* takes place when we fail to acknowledge our basic rights and do not go after our needs and wants. We remain silent or say things are all right when actually they are not. Aggressive people seek out nonassertive people because they know they will receive few complaints from them.
Nonassertive employees don't reveal their thinking, may even suffer in silence, and will move to another department without confronting issues in their present job. They might have a bright idea but won't volunteer it for fear of being ridiculed. They are poor time managers because they can never truly be in control of themselves or their jobs. *Assertiveness* takes place when we acknowledge the importance of our thoughts, feelings, and desires, and communicate them to others firmly, clearly, and affirmatively when appropriate. *Assertive communication saves time*

because it is clear and to the point. Assertive people are in control because they know what they want and try to obtain it in the most direct way possible. Assertiveness is courteous. The moment I become discourteous to you, I have put you down so now I become aggressive in the negative sense.

To make the distinction, a manager who is disturbed constantly by a staff member can communicate on any one of the three levels. The aggressive manager says: "Jones, can't you see I'm busy? Come and see me later." The nonassertive manager says nothing and lets Jones interrupt. The assertive manager says: "David, I'm concentrating on a report just now and the interruptions upset my train of thought. Please gather all your questions and we will deal with them at 11." The overly aggressive manager causes resentment in the staff member. The nonassertive manager feels resentful toward the staff member. The assertive manager gives little reason for resentment and deals with the problem immediately in as pleasant a manner as possible.

The Use of the I-Message in Assertiveness

The I-message is the most direct form of assertive communication.

"John, I would like to use that typewriter within the next half hour. Is that O.K.?"

The you-message is aggressive, causing resentment.

"John, you've been at that typewriter a long time and I need it."

The next 15 minutes could be spent in conflict—perhaps the next 2 days!

Let's look at the conversation of two assertive people using the I-message formula.

"John, I would like to use that typewriter within the next half hour. Is that O.K.?"

"I have planned to use it steadily for the next 2 hours, Alan. How long will you need it?"

"About 20 minutes."

"My report is urgent and I doubt if I can spare 20 minutes. Can you wait or use another typewriter?"

"McDonald wants me to use this typewriter and wants this quickly. What if I ask him which has to be done first?"

"O.K. Alan, I agree. I think this kind of thing happens too often, though. I would like you and I and McDonald to sit down and work out a solution for the future."

Notice that these people both reveal their thoughts. They work toward a solution. They do not accuse each other or get into the conflict of "mine is more important than yours." They refuse to become emotionally involved over the use of a typewriter and save time by making a decision quickly.

Look at these four ways in which you can be assertive and which can save you time and energy.

1. *Ask relevant questions.* Never assume. Mistakes are made daily in most business because one person "thought" that the other person wanted the job done a certain way. When you are not sure, make sure by asking. We often find an inner voice saying "Now you should know that. Won't you look silly if you have to go and ask her. She'll think the answer is so obvious and she'll probably put you down for asking." Fortunately, most managers are grateful that employees want to have matters clarified, but even when we ask someone who might ridicule us for the question, is it not better to receive the right information than to go and do the job erroneously? Learn also that the person who ridicules has a problem, not the one who is ridiculed. Do not accept the ridicule, which brings us to the next consideration.

2. *Confront with gentleness.* An enormous amount of time is taken up harboring resentment or feeling the other person is wrong. When you have a problem with someone you work with let that person know about it, otherwise you'll avoid the person (and the work won't get done) or may talk about the person to others, creating a negative atmosphere. Use the I-message when confronting. It is more gentle and likely to win positive results. Keep from accusing. Instead of:

"You always leave me out. Everyone else on the staff gets to know what's going on and I don't."

You can say:

"I have a problem, Susan. I don't seem to get the information I need from you and I would like 5 minutes of your time to talk about it."

Ask for time to discuss a problem. This means you can be more "collected" and it indicates the serious nature of the problem to you.

People who come up front and confront gently are normally trusted and respected and receive promotion. This will not happen, of course, in a company or agency that is basically dishonest.

You can confront superiors in your company as long as you show that you are being positive in what you want to accomplish.

3. *Be ready to say "No."* If you are a "nice guy" who does for everyone, you encourage slackness in others and you ruin your own time managing. Your daily list and priority setting will go out the window unless you decline requests. There are orders from higher up that must be answered with a "yes," of course, and you will know when you have no option. But in most cases, you can refuse to do what may be other people's work. We all carry around signs for others to read. The signs are not pinned on our coats; they are to be read in our words, body language, and tone. Some of us carry around a sign that says "I want you to like me. If I can do anything to help you, ask me." We invite abuse if our signal to others indicates that we can be abused. (By the way, the "never-say-no" person is generally liked but not respected. He or she consequently feels resentful for the lack of respect.)

4. *Volunteer your ideas.* If you have a suggestion, make it known. Don't discount your own ideas. If you feel scared about rejection, think of the objections to your idea first and answer them in your own mind before volunteering your idea.

If you see an employee taking half an hour to do a 15-minute job, let that person know how he or she can do it quicker. Use the I-message again. Tell the employee how you learned to do it and how you found it quicker. People respond well as long as they don't feel accused or are made to feel small.

Making suggestions saves time. When the boss tells you to do a job and how to do it and you know how to do it quicker, ask if there is any special reason why he or she wants you to do it that way. If there is none, give your suggestion. The boss is no more or less a fallible human being than yourself. There is no disrespect in suggesting another way to top-level management.

If your ideas are constantly stifled ask yourself these questions.

1. Am I communicating in a positive manner? Is there a possibility I am making them feel small by my suggestion?

2. Does top management really want to change? (Even though they have a "token" suggestion box to make it look good!) What about asking why my suggestions are constantly blocked? Who would be likely to be most honest with me?

3. Am I in the company best suited to me? (The company that operates with the board or president making all the changes will not satisfy a creative employee. He or she works best in a structure that welcomes creativity.)

Assertiveness pays off in terms of time, productivity, and promotion. Test yourself to see where you stand. Write down the names of people you work with (include all levels) and check the appropriate column opposite.

NAME	I ASK QUESTIONS WHEN APPROPRIATE			I CONFRONT WHEN NEEDED			I SAY NO WHEN I SHOULD			I VOLUNTEER IDEAS WHEN APPROPRIATE		
	nearly always	some-times	rarely	nearly always	some-times	rarely	nearly always	some-times	rarely	nearly always	some-times	rarely

CHAPTER 13
THE NEED FOR A POSITIVE WORK ATMOSPHERE

So you have a new idea you would like the whole staff to adopt? You would like to introduce a 2-hour quiet time? You need others to cooperate with you on an important project?

You might be the high-level manager who can say what is going to be done, but it will be the employees who will make it all happen, or make it all not happen. The degree of success rests with the attitude of the staff toward the job.

Frederick Hertzberg, renowned for his studies on human behavior within organizations, has already shown us that people are not motivated to work well simply because the office is well furnished and the pay is reasonable. People need to feel important in their jobs for optimum cooperation to take place, and the manager can help provide the kind of atmosphere that makes people feel important. He or she must help build a positive work atmosphere. Here are four ways to do it:

1. *Be assertive.* (Consult previous chapter.) Assertive behavior is always positive. The atmosphere becomes honest. Assertiveness is catching, particularly when you give permission to your staff to be the same as yourself. Encourage people to speak up.

2. *Listen carefully* to your staff. Schedule consultations at the right time of day. Make eye contact. Take notes of what they suggest. Provide feedback. Ask questions for clarification. This is *creative* listening. When you merely say, "Oh yeah" or "I understand" as you usher them out the door, you are into *passive listening.* People feel discounted through passive listening.

3. *Give appropriate recognition.* Look for improvement in work habits and tell your staff member what you see. Do it often. Do it everyday to at least one staff member. Form the pleasant habit of praising your people. Do you know if your secretary is typing faster and with less mistakes than 6 months ago? You don't know? You do know but haven't mentioned it? What an opportunity you have missed to build a positive work atmosphere!

It is easier to give negative feedback when you have already acknowledged positive aspects of a person's work. The question should be asked when giving negative feedback (criticism) "Does this person consider that I'm 'for' or 'against' him or her in giving this criticism?" The person will consider that you're "for" him or her if you have already acknowledged his or her work in a positive fashion.

Try to give five positives to every one negative! Avoid "You're doing a good job, but—." No one really hears when you say the first part of your sentence! Spell out what it is you find good about your staff member. "You're doing a good job" is too vague.

The yearly evaluation you give your employee will never be a surprise if you keep feeding positives and negatives regularly.

4. *Take time to laugh.* Work is not one big joke, but it is a place where people spend most of their waking hours, Monday through Friday. If the office is a very serious place people become depressed. If you go around with a plastic smile on your face all day long, people become disgusted.

Simply be a human being with your staff. Employees generally become uptight when they are working with a superstar kind of manager. If they can feel relaxed with you, they will cooperate.

A positive work atmosphere brings about a *team spirit*, *more productivity*, *less absenteeism*, and *less time waste*.

THE NEED FOR A POSITIVE WORK ATMOSPHERE 97

ACTION PLAN

What I am aware of now (or more fully) through this workshop.

Skills I have learned in this course.

What I would like to do as a result of this course.

ITEM	HOW I COULD IMPLEMENT IT	WHEN I PLAN TO START

BIBLIOGRAPHY

Fensterheim, Herbert, & Baer, Jean. *Don't say yes when you want to say no.* New York: Dell, 1975.

Gordon, Thomas. *P.E.T. (parent effectiveness training).* New York: Wyden, 1970.

Jongeward, Dorothy, & Scott, Dru. *Affirmative action for women.* Menlo Park, Calif.: Addison-Wesley, 1973.

Jongeward, Dorothy. *Everybody wins.* Menlo Park, Calif.: Addison-Wesley, 1973.

Lakein, Alan. *How to get control of your time and your life.* New York: Wyden, 1973.

Mackenzie, R. Alec. *The time trap.* New York: McGraw-Hill, 1972.

Webber, Ross A. *Time and management.* New York: Van Nostrand Reinhold, 1972.

Notes

Notes

Notes

Notes

Notes

Notes